mexicanmodern

new food from mexico

mexicanmodern

new food from mexico

FIONA DUNLOP

photographs by Jean-Blaise Hall

Interlink Books

An imprint of Interlink Publishing Group, Inc.
Northampton, Massachusetts

First published in the United States in 2009 by

INTERLINK BOOKS
An imprint of Interlink Publishing Group, Inc.
46 Crosby Street
Northampton, Massachusetts 01060
www.interlinkbooks.com

ISBN 978 1 56656 744 2

Commissioning Editor Rebecca Spry
Art Director Tim Foster
Jacket Design Juliana Spear
Designer Nicky Collings
Photographer Jean-Blaise Hall
Recipe Translator Ana Sims
Project Editor Georgina Atsiaris
Editor Debbie Robertson
Production Lucy Carter; Sara Rauch
Proofreader Kate Parker
Food Consultant Hiltrud Schulz
Americanization Sara Rauch
Indexer Diana LeCore

Printed and bound in China

Acknowledgments

Much of the impetus for this challenging project came from Manuel Díaz Cebrián, the dynamic head of the Mexican Tourist Office in London – to him a huge thank you, and also to Luis Rendón-Aguilar for his patience and logistical support, together with the Segretaria de Turismo in Mexico City.

Out there in that bewitching country of Mexico, my thanks go to all the chefs who collaborated so willingly, spared precious time, and put up with our questions, cameras, and appetites. How lucky I was to meet them and of course indulge in their divine dishes.

It was a pleasure to travel with my collaborators: Ana Sims, the recipe translator, who worked communication wonders, and Jean-Blaise Hall, the photographer, whose enthusiasm carried us through thick and thin. My gratitude, too, to chef David Sterling in Mérida for his tips, great memories of supping Aztec chocolate with Héctor del Puerto in Condesa, and immense appreciation of all the generous-spirited people encountered on the road, in kitchens, and in markets.

Back in the UK, my thanks go to the designer, Nicky Collings, for her warmth, keenness, and vision, to Georgina Atsiaris for her patience, and as always to my commissioning editor, Becca Spry. Deafening applause, too, for Juan Galindo, whom I consulted for his expertise on Mexican food, and for my old friend Jessica Johnson who introduced me to Mexico many aeons ago (in memory of VWs, pyramids, ant-bears, and the like).

Finally, Richard: he knows how much I appreciate his constant support – but thank you.

contents

5

INTRODUCTION

Mexico thrives on radicalism. The very word revolution conjures up the incredible vitality of a country where conflicts and political upheavals have peppered the calendar since pre-Hispanic days. The latest mutation is quite different, however, as it is all about a strengthening of national identity, or *Mexicanidad* (Mexican-ness). Visible in a resurgent avant-garde culture, nourished by Mexico's baroque imagination and deep soul, a new confidence is permeating every field from cinema to music and art, placing Mexico firmly on the creative world map. Not least, it is transforming the food.

With immense flair, modern chefs now combine extraordinary native flavors with a sophisticated sense of balance and presentation. By layering rare, ambrosial flavors in presentations of sheer poetry, Mexican chefs are hitting the headlines: the gastro *revolución* is upon us! Yet rather than a revolution, it has been an evolution. What is happening is a complete reappraisal of food traditions that had come to be regarded as old-fashioned and even backward. The variety of Mexico's regional cuisines is huge, with 62 distinct indigenous groups thriving mainly in the center and south. Many feature in this book, beside other extraordinary recipes found on our epicurean path. From dynamic Mexico City to an eccentric hill village in Veracruz, to the traditional university towns of Morelia and Puebla, to the strongly indigenous Oaxaca and finally, to Mayan territory in the Yucatán.

Whether up in the dry sierra or down on the tropical coast, some of the tastiest local food is found in markets, from the gamut of corn-based snacks such as *tostadas*, *tacos*, *chalupas*, *panuchos*, *esquites*, and *uchepos*, to countless regional specialities. The big change is that refined versions of these classics are now gracing the white tablecloths of Mexico's ritziest restaurants.

Chilies are omnipresent, but their balance is being orchestrated more delicately. Tender *nopales* (cactus leaves) sneak into sophisticated salads, earthy *huitlacoche* (corn fungus) is revered as the Mexican truffle, *pepitas* (pumpkin seeds) adorn meats, and silky yellow zucchini flowers blossom *ad infinitum*. Then there are the "new" hallmarks of the herb-and-spice department: *hoja santa*, a large aromatic leaf used to flavor or wrap fish and *tamales*; allspice berries; *amaranto* grains and leaves; dark red *achiote* seeds, and an indefinable herb, *epazote*.

So far, innovative chefs have eschewed more extreme native fauna such as armadillo (a pork-like meat still popular in the Isthmus and Chiapas) and iguana (very big in Isthmus markets), although sustainably farmed iguana could well be the next low-fat alternative to chicken – it certainly tastes like it. What chefs have embraced with enthusiasm are pre-Hispanic fowl and game such as duck, turkey, and venison, moving away from the Old World stalwarts of beef, lamb, and pork.

Desserts, other than the cake and sweet production of the convents, were never a Mexican forte as sugar had no place in the indigenous diet, but even that is changing. Nor can you sing the praises of Mexico's beers too highly, from sunny Corona to golden Pacifico to the dark Yucatecan brew, León. Then there are the smooth, upgraded tequilas and, hard on their heels, estate-bottled *mezcales*, which sometimes slip into the cooking pan. Mexico's palate-tantalizing riches seem infinite.

THE WORLD'S FIRST FUSION FOOD

The Spaniards landed in Veracruz in 1519 a few decades after the Moors' 800-year-long occupation of Spain. The Moorish imprint was still evident in the spices, citrus fruit, and rice that were brought to Mexico. As the climate of

central Mexico resembled that of the Mediterranean, imports adapted well; cattle for meat and dairy products, wheat, sugar cane, apples, onions, and herbs all flourished. Then a vital culinary change occurred with pork, lard, and subsequently frying. This was a completely new departure for the indigenous Mexicans. Until then, cooking entailed either boiling, steaming, or for the Mayas, smoking and baking in underground pits. Even salt was not used; instead they added the mineral *tequesquite.*

From sugar came sweets and cakes, something the nuns of Puebla excelled at when not laboring over their complex *moles,* and from Seville oranges came Yucatecan marinades. Further foreign input came when Spanish galleons sailed directly across the Pacific to unload Oriental bounty at Acapulco. Sesame seeds, cinnamon, garlic, and cilantro were all introduced through the back door. In reverse, Mexico gave Old Europe chilies, tomatoes, avocados,

pumpkins, turkey, vanilla, and, of course, chocolate, that divine tipple supped by the Aztec emperor Moctezuma from a cup of solid gold after a typical 30-course dinner.

With all this, Mexican cuisine is a revelation. It is an assault of subtle, smoky, sometimes fiery but always exotic flavors and textures that are completely foreign to Old World palates and light-years from Tex-Mex. Flour is hardly ever used for making sauces; in its place there are salsas, *moles* or *pipianes* (rich, complex, thickened purées), *adobos* (sour marinades), and *recados* (Mayan seasoning). In fact, Mexican cooking is considered to be one of the world's three original cuisines, along with those of China and France.

It is also one of the most documented, inspiring reams of academic investigations, seminars, and ponderous columns in the Mexican press. The initiator was Bernardino de Sahagun (1499–1590), a Franciscan missionary who,

after becoming fluent in Nahuatl, the language of the Aztecs, compiled the *Florentine Codex*. This documented Aztec society and culture, including its food. Other observations came from Bernal Díaz (1496–1584), a captain in the army of Hernán Cortés and author of *The Conquest of New Spain* (1568). More recently the inspired theorist José Iturriaga de la Fuente headed a massive state-funded investigation into Mexico's regional market food. And on a more lyrical note, Laura Esquivel's magic-realist book *Like Water for Chocolate* (1989) and eponymous film (1992) did much to romanticize Mexican cuisine. Who can forget Tita's lovingly prepared quail with rose petals?

CORN WORSHIP

Some things just do not change. Take corn (maize), the staff of Mexican life that is thought to have been cultivated from wild grass 6,000–7,000 years ago, making it man's first feat of genetic engineering. For all Mexicans, corn is sacred: 300 million corn *tortillas* are consumed daily (not counting the wheat ones conquering northern Mexico). The Mayas believed man was made of corn while the Mexicas (ancestors of the Aztecs) said their god of corn, Centéotl, was born in Michoacán, "land of water and humidity." *Tortillas* ("little cakes") were named as such by the Spaniards when they first tasted the corn flat bread. After decades of being replaced in upmarket restaurants by crusty bread rolls, *tortillas* are hip again, although they never disappeared from domestic kitchens or the markets. Vital but labor-intensive energy-givers, they are estimated to have monopolized 35–40 hours a week of a pre-Hispanic woman's time. No Aztec man would be seen dead with a *metate* and *mano* (lava stone rolling table and rolling pin) or *molcajete* and *tejolote* (mortar and pestle), the unrivaled kitchen equipment that are still widely used.

CHILIES, THE SECRET WEAPON

Mexican cuisine is often perceived as chili-hot in the extreme. This is rarely the case: when the heat of a chili, such as the *habanero*, comes close to shooting off the Scoville scale (the universal measure of capsaicin, or chili fieriness; see page 184), it is incorporated into a salsa, so it can be carefully rationed. What is true is that chilies are addictive: once tasted, never forgotten. Some 200 varieties exist but the most common ones boil down to a dozen or so, including *ancho, mulato,* and *pasilla,* the holy trinity of *moles.* Mexican cooks are adept at building up complex flavors by combining different varieties or by blending fresh, dried, and smoked chilies. Each region has its favorite chilies and, like corn, some are unique to one area. To confuse matters further, names change according to whether the chilies are fresh, smoked, and/or dried: a dried *poblano* chili, for example, becomes an *ancho,* and the popular *chipotle* is really a smoked and dried *jalapeño.* Like Mexico's other primary foods, the chili goes back thousands of years. One recent archaeological find identified ten varieties of 1500-year-old chilies in a cave – remnants of an ancient *mole?*

INSTINCTIVE NUTRITION

The native Mexican diet incorporated remarkable nutritional balance. For example, the amino acid levels in corn and beans complement each other perfectly; *nopales* (cactus leaves) contain abundant vitamins A, C, B complex, and iron; and avocados contribute nearly 20 different vitamins and minerals. Fresh chilies are high in vitamin C while dried ones clock up loads of vitamin A. *Amaranto* seed, the "new" superfood, which is packed with protein, calcium, iron, vitamin E, and lycine, had great ritualistic significance for the Aztecs.

Even the hallowed *masa harina* (corn flour), the basis of *tortillas,* is bursting with calcium after the corn kernels have been soaked then slow-cooked with lime or wood ash. Fresh fruit juices mixed on street corners are now an art in themselves. In view of this, it is doubly tragic that Mexico is now the world's greatest consumer of Coca-Cola, with the Yucatán at the top of the class. Compare that with the vitamin C rich *agua de jamaica* (hibiscus flower juice).

Today's *nueva cocina* is fighting a tough battle against processed and convenience products, mainly imported from the US and the globalized markets. Yet with innovative, energetic chefs from Mexico City to Michoacán, Puebla to Veracruz and Oaxaca to the Yucatán leading the way, the word is spreading. Regional food is more popular than ever and has become emperor again, although with completely transformed presentation and an inimitable Mexican touch:

poetry, magic, the whisper of the gods? But ultimately, when you stand on a street-corner, sniff the air and scent that unmistakable aroma of corn, whether from *tacos, elotes,* or *tostadas*, you know for sure you are in Mexico.

méxico d.f.

Love it or hate it, Mexico City (Mexico D.F.) never fails to electrify. Vast scales and extremes, heaving intensity, a black-faced Virgen de Guadalupe: it has it all. High on a plateau rimmed by volcanoes, the city's tentacular spread encompasses over 22 million people. Out of this maelstrom comes extraordinary dynamism that generates inspired art and hard-hitting cinema at the same time as violence and political unrest. Then there is the food. While traffic surges down the main axes between purple jacaranda trees, avant-garde sculptures, and towering office-blocks, backstreets are lined with makeshift food-kitchens, their smoke curling into the air. Even on the huge *zócalo* (main square) fronting the cathedral and presidential palace, vendors cook up pungent, sizzling local fare.

Nothing encapsulates the social extremes of the city better than its gastronomy. You can dine exquisitely in minimalist chic in Polanco, the upscale business district, lounge with hip *chilangos* (inhabitants of the capital) on a restaurant terrace in leafy Condesa, snack on grasshoppers in the old historic center, or wolf down a *taco* in a far-flung *barrio* (neighborhood). Food is everywhere, as food means life, and has for centuries since *tianguis* (markets) were the economic motor of the powerful Aztec empire. In 1325, the Aztecs built their capital, Tenochtitlan (now Mexico City), over a vast lake. Causeways connected villages and elaborately painted pyramids rose between waterways and floating gardens. The magnificent city inspired the conquistador diarist, Bernal Díaz, to describe it as "an enchanted vision," while four centuries later Diego Rivera, the painter husband of Frida Kahlo, celebrated the Aztec culture in his fabulous murals. Only a miniature version survives today in Xochimilco, on the southern edge, where canoes and gondolas navigate between *chinampas* (floating nursery-gardens) and verdant banks. Ear-shattering *mariachi* serenades mark the time difference.

Something close to an enchanted foodie vision can be found just east of the city center at La Merced, the capital's labyrinthine market. Said to trade over 24,000 tons of fruit and vegetables daily, it is housed in gigantic hangars where produce spills out onto surrounding streets in a veritable cornucopia. Watching over activities from a neighboring church, the serene patron saint, the Virgen de la Merced, allows stallholders just one day off a year on her festival, September 24. Otherwise the market functions from sunrise to sunset, intermeshing work and life in a seamless flow. Following the Aztec pattern, specialist sections offer dozens of types of produce. Fresh, smoked, or sun-dried chilies dominate one side; farther in, men fold mountains of banana-leaves while others prepare cylindrical stacks of *nopales* (cactus leaves); then there are *tomatillos* in papery skins, fiery-orange papayas, fragrant guavas, sunny mangoes, truckfuls of corn ears, enough avocados for a million guacamoles, zingy-yellow zucchini flowers, sacks of dried beans, and huge scarlet watermelons. Men and women stir gigantic earthenware *cazuelas* (casseroles) or slap and toss *tortillas* on *comales* (hotplates).

Such basic food rituals are timeless, but in other parts of the city the 21st-century zeitgeist rules. For decades, most of the capital's upscale restaurants dished up that crashing misnomer, "international cuisine," with its tedious imitations of French classics. This was a hangover from the long dictatorship (1877–1911) of Porfirio Díaz, a general ingrained with Old World pretensions who came to power soon after a bizarre Gallic reign. This was fronted by Emperor Maximilian and his wife, Carlota, both hapless puppets of Napoleon III. The result was a gastronomic and social paradox, with the working classes scoffing healthy beans, pumpkin, avocado, tomatoes, and corn, washed down by juices or, on a bad day, *pulque* (a type of beer made from the fermented juice of the maguey plant), while the bourgeoisie indulged in heavy cream sauces and imported wines and spirits. Virtually the only shared Mexican elements were chilies and *tortillas*, although even French bread had appeared along with *potages*, thanks to Carlota.

Despite the Mexican Revolution of 1910, which toppled Díaz, little changed on the food front until the late 1980s when nutritional concerns, combined with a revival of indigenous ingredients, followed the trail blazed by France's *nouvelle cuisine* and the Spanish example. In fact, Spain's groundbreaking *nueva cocina* chef, Juan Mari Arzak of San Sebastian, now has a restaurant in the Zona Rosa.

Many of Mexico City's pioneering chefs have been women. Patricia Quintana, Alicia Gironella de'Angeli, Carmen Ramírez, Mónica Patiño; all set out to serve healthy fare rooted in their culture. This produced native turkey, duck, or rabbit cooked in aromatic leaves like *hoja santa*, or served with delicate zucchini flowers and insects. *Huitlacoche* (corn truffle), too, made a resounding comeback from the sizzling *comales* (hotplates) of market *taquerías* (*taco* stalls) to the porcelain plates of high cuisine. As the 21st-century progresses, a younger generation with direct experience of international gastronomic trends is starting to wield the pans. Presentation is now paramount, though ingredients remain Mexican. But this is Mexico City, specialist in extremes, so it really is a case of "watch this (very large) space."

martha ortiz
aguila y sol

There is no doubt about it, Martha Ortiz is the *pasionaria* of Mexico's top chefs. Steeped in poetry, history, art, and large doses of black coffee, she combines these inspirational threads (minus the coffee) in her food. Your plate can easily contain hibiscus flowers or zucchini blossoms, while a slice of star fruit and a tiny mint leaf float in your glass of water. Japanese haiku come to mind, but then suddenly Mexico returns as chili punches its way through, followed by a mysterious pre-Hispanic plant called *huauzontle* (a green vegetable similar to broccoli) and fish cooked on an open flame.

"For me every dish is a small story. I want to cook my idea of Mexico," enthuses Martha, a striking, raven-haired charmer in her 40s. "Food is an integral part of beauty – that's something I absorbed from my upbringing as my mother loves cooking. As a child, I fantasized about people eating. We weren't allowed to watch TV so my imagination was fed by books. Of course I always wanted to be Anna Karenina as opposed to Madame Bovary!" This statement is typical of a woman who seems to be playing a role in her own highly complex drama in which each idea leapfrogs the next.

Although she started off studying political science and Mexican history, Martha soon realized her heart was in the kitchen, so her next stop was a cookery school in Mexico City. "I've always preferred making food to actually eating it," she insists. Her path also led her to work abroad in graphic design before her first marriage to a painter. "But his pictures always came first," she groans. "So we divorced!" Despite this, Martha loves art and offers the lobby space below her restaurant to young artists. Even the elevator has a mini-installation of books: "It gives the place energy and dynamism."

Martha is evidently a diva, both adored and feared by her staff. Theatrical she may be, but her passion is catching as she gesticulates, laughs, and talks. Then, suddenly, she will ask, "What's the flavor of love?" This, you learn, is because her next "concept" menu will have love as a theme.

"When I think of a new dish I make drawings, which are technically horrible," she giggles. "And then I think up the names – that's important. They can be poetic or funny. I love using poems in my concept menus." A future menu will be about magic, she announces. "I want to go up into the sierra with a woman shaman – into the hills of Oaxaca or Michoacán."

Her boundless energy inevitably affects her working hours. "I don't need much sleep – four hours is enough – so I leave the restaurant late. My second husband got so fed up that one day he gave me an ultimatum. It wasn't difficult to choose." She smiles winningly and you know that she has no regrets.

chilled cream of avocado soup
crema fría de aguacate con semilla ceremonial

Martha creates a dish the like of which you will have never tasted before. Aromatic herbs contrast with hot chili, subtle avocado with coconut, sweet potato with crisp apple. Use plain shredded coconut if you can't find the chili-flavored version. For a sharper flavor, add a spoonful of white wine vinegar.

In a food processor, blend the avocado, chilies, sour cream, coconut milk, and chicken stock. Add the coriander seeds, oregano, and salt to taste. Strain and refrigerate until chilled.

To make the sweet potato fritters, heat ½in (1cm) of oil in a frying pan over high heat. When the oil is hot, add the sweet potato slices and reduce heat to medium. Slowly fry the sweet potato slices until just golden and slightly crisp. Remove from the oil and lay on paper towels to absorb the excess oil.

To make the oregano vinaigrette, whisk the vinegar with the mustard and season with salt and pepper. Add the dried and fresh oregano, then the olive oil and beat to blend well.

Serve the chilled soup in individual bowls, topped with a splash of oregano vinaigrette, diced apple and cucumber, a couple of sweet potato fritters, and a sprinkling of chili-flavored coconut.

serves 6

- 2 large avocados, about 1lb (450g), peeled and pitted
- 1½ *serrano* chilies
- 2 tbsp sour cream
- 3½ fl oz (100ml) coconut milk
- 10fl oz (300ml) chicken stock
- 1½ tsp coriander seeds, crushed
- ¼ tsp dried oregano
- salt, to taste
- 2oz (55g) green apple, cored and diced
- 2oz (55g) cucumber, peeled and diced
- 1 tbsp chili-flavored shredded coconut

for the sweet potato fritters

- 1 sweet potato, peeled and thinly sliced
- vegetable, corn, or peanut oil

for the oregano vinaigrette

- 2 tbsp white wine vinegar
- 1 tsp Dijon mustard
- salt and finely ground white pepper
- 2 tsp dried oregano
- 1 tbsp finely chopped fresh oregano (or sage)
- 4fl oz (125ml) olive oil

"nationalist" guacamole
guacamole nacionalista

This is a Martha Ortiz trademark dish, as the colors of the dish represent her beloved Mexican flag: green, red, and white. The pomegranate ping makes a great addition to this classic appetizer. The dish is easy to make and will keep in the fridge for a few hours covered with plastic wrap to avoid discoloring. Serve with *tortilla* chips or toasted pita bread.

Marinate the onion in the lemon juice for half an hour, then drain and set aside.

Mash the avocado and add the cilantro, marinated onion, and *serrano* chilies. Season with salt and pepper.

Make a mound of guacamole on a serving plate and scatter over the pomegranate seeds and ricotta.

serves 6

2 large onions, peeled and finely chopped

15fl oz (425ml) fresh lemon juice

4 large avocados, about 1lb 14oz (850g), peeled and pitted

4oz (115g) chopped fresh cilantro leaves

3oz (85g) *serrano* chilies, seeded, deveined, and chopped

salt and freshly ground black pepper

1oz (30g) fresh pomegranate seeds

2oz (55g) ricotta, crumbled

star tuna with vegetable streamers
atún estrella de mar de verduras

To make the spice coating, mix together all the ingredients in a large bowl.

To infuse the herb oil, slowly cook the garlic in a large saucepan of the oil over low heat until golden. Remove from the heat and allow to cool slightly. Add the chilies, thyme, rosemary, bay leaves, and pepper and stir to mix.

To prepare the vinaigrette, whisk together the mustard, vinegars, and sugar in a bowl until well blended and season with salt and pepper. Combine the corn and olive oils and slowly whisk into the mustard mixture until well blended. Continue to whisk while adding one and a half tablespoons of water. Marinate the sugar beet and carrots in the vinaigrette while preparing the tuna.

To make the sesame oil, mix together all the ingredients and blend well.

Completely coat the tuna in the spice coating, then carefully dip into the herb oil. Sear briefly over high heat to seal all over.

Cut the tuna into thin slices and arrange on individual serving plates. Garnish with a few marinated vegetable streamers, a drizzle of sesame oil, and a sprinkling of sesame seeds and *jalapeño* chilies.

serves 6

6oz (175g) sugar beet, peeled and cut into thin strips

6oz (175g) carrots, cut into thin strips

1lb 5oz (600g) yellow-fin tuna loin, trimmed into neat rounds

1 tbsp black sesame seeds, to garnish

2 *jalapeño* chilies, seeded, deveined, and cut into thin strips, to garnish

for the spice coating

3 tbsp each white pepper, black pepper, ground ginger, and ground *piquin* chili

4 tbsp paprika

1 tbsp salt, or to taste

for the herb oil

5 cloves of garlic, peeled and crushed

1 pint (600ml) olive oil

4 dried *arbol* chilies

1½ tsp chopped fresh thyme leaves

1 tbsp chopped fresh rosemary

10 bay leaves

1 tsp freshly ground black pepper

for the vinaigrette

1 tsp Dijon mustard

1 tbsp each white wine vinegar, balsamic vinegar, and brown sugar

salt and finely ground white pepper

2½ fl oz (75ml) each corn oil and olive oil

for the sesame oil

1½ tbsp spicy sesame oil

2½ fl oz (75ml) olive oil

1 tbsp light soy sauce

1½ tsp safflower oil

The bottom line of this quite divine dish is the herb oil infused with the extra-hot and smoky-flavored *arbol* chili. The recipe requires a lot of advance preparation but the end result is out of this world, amalgamating sweet, salty, tart, hot, and sour in a real *tour de force*.

caramelized mamey cream
crema de mamey estofada a la hoja de oro

This princely dessert looks and tastes exquisite. The orange flesh of the tropical mamey fruit is smooth, creamy, sweet, and rich in vitamins A and C. If you cannot find mamey fruit, use mango or even firm peaches instead.

In a saucepan, heat the whipping cream with half the sugar and the mamey flesh. Bring to a boil and immediately remove from heat. Leave to cool.

Beat the egg yolks with the rest of the sugar until completely blended. Stir in some of the cooled mamey cream until well blended, then add the rest and mix well. Put the mixture in a blender, whizz to a purée, then strain and spoon off the foam.

Preheat the oven to 225°F/110°C. Pour the mamey purée into individual baking dishes and sit these in a roasting pan. Pour in some nearly boiling water to come at least halfway up the sides of the dishes. Bake for about 18 minutes until set. Remove from the oven, allow to cool, and refrigerate.

Meanwhile, make the carnation syrup. Pour 5fl oz (150ml) of water into a small saucepan, stir in the sugar, and simmer for 30 minutes over medium heat. Remove from the heat and allow to cool. Stir in the grenadine, violet concentrate, and carnation petal. The syrup should have the consistency of thick honey. Adding a few drops of lemon juice will give an extra kick.

Before serving, sprinkle some brown sugar over the top of the mamey creams and place under a broiler to caramelize. Garnish each dish with a gold leaf and a few carnation petals, and serve with a drizzle of carnation syrup.

serves 4

14fl oz (400ml) whipping cream

3 tbsp granulated sugar

5oz (140g) mamey or mango, peeled, pitted, and diced

4 egg yolks

4oz (115g) brown sugar

4 edible gold leaves (optional), to garnish

fresh organic carnations, to garnish

for the carnation syrup

2½oz (70g) superfine sugar

1 tsp grenadine syrup

1 tsp violet concentrate

1 fresh organic carnation petal

1 tsp fresh lemon juice (optional)

Mexico's *aguas* (literally "waters") are legion and perfect for hot summer days. As the natural fruit juice is diluted with water and spiked with other flavors, it is extremely refreshing. Martha's versions are, of course, ultra-sophisticated – pure liquid poetry.

hibiscus flower water with rose petals
agua de jamaica con caricia de rosas

serves 4

9fl oz (250ml) hibiscus flower tea

6fl oz (175ml) simple syrup

5 tsp each cinnamon, clove, and star aniseed herbal tea

1¼ pints (700ml) of mineral water

8 ice cubes, or to taste

edible rose petals, to garnish

zest of 1 orange, cut into matchsticks, to garnish (optional)

Mix all the ingredients in a glass pitcher and stir. Garnish with rose petals and orange matchsticks.

lemon water with mint
agua fresca de limón con hierbabuena

serves 4

24 large mint leaves

1¼ pints (700ml) mineral water, sparkling or still

4fl oz (125ml) lemon juice

4fl oz (125ml) simple syrup

8 ice cubes, or to taste

4 slices of lemon, to garnish

In a blender, whiz the mint leaves with 18fl oz (500ml) of the mineral water. Strain. Stir in the lemon juice, simple syrup, and the rest of the water, then add the ice. Decorate each glass with a slice of lemon.

mónica patiño
naos

Mónica Patiño is Mexico City's proverbial wonderwoman. Creative chef, wife, mother of four, TV host, and cookbook author, she runs three highly regarded restaurants and an organic grocery. Then suddenly she announces she is off on a Buddhist retreat. Although not what you might expect from the head of a burgeoning gastro-empire, if you look closely you can see the harmony in Mónica's features, and it is reflected in the beautiful food she creates.

Her unique fusion of Mexican and Asian food, with a touch of Europe, comes from years of hard work following the opening of her first restaurant in the Valle de Bravo in 1978. Other ventures followed in Mexico City, including the Oriental-style haven, MP Café + Bistro. Then in 2004 Naos burst onto the scene. Although the name refers to Ancient Egyptian shrines, the curved, glassed-in terrace and sleek interior embody a sophisticated Mexico City, typical of the Polanco location.

At 5:30pm lingering lunchers may include her father, a distinguished-looking retired banker who, with her brother, is her business-partner. Mónica readily admits to the importance of her family. "My father's a real gourmet, I must have caught the bug from him. He traveled a lot for his job and became very discerning about different cuisines." Mónica's emotional warmth is contagious, extending to the kitchen that hums with good humor, laughter, and the odd song.

So how did this well-bred *chilanga*, born and bred in the capital, come to cooking? "When I was 18 I had two parallel paths," she explains thoughtfully. "I was a bit of a rebel but was also looking for spiritual direction. When I found food, I realized that it could be a way of practicing and integrating the spiritual side.

"During my teens I often went to Europe and even went to a school in Llandudno for a year – I chose it because of the Beatles," she laughs. "That's where I discovered marmalade and steak and kidney pie, which I still love! Then, in the early 1980s, the French chef Guy Savoy invited me to train at his new restaurant in Paris. He was a real magician and the king of *nouvelle cuisine* at that time. It was here I saw a Japanese sous-chef preparing vegetables." This was Mónica's epiphany. "I decided to go to Asia to learn to cook without cream, delicately, to make translucent sauces.

"My first visit there was a shock, it was like another planet. Since then I've spent time in Thailand and Myanmar, and India, of course, and even made a pilgrimage to Mount Kailash" (a remote and sacred peak in the Himalayas). Talking to her, watching her work in the kitchen and seeing her dedication, you realize she has brilliantly integrated her philosophy on life with her cooking. The result on the plate is its incarnation, in this life at least.

Relatively easy to prepare, yet spiked with contrasting flavors, this vegetarian terrine makes a great summer appetizer or informal lunch. The eggplant was brought to Mexico by the Spaniards, but red peppers are truly indigenous. Advance salting helps reduce the amount of oil the eggplant absorbs during cooking.

eggplant and goat's cheese mosaic
mosaico de berenjena y queso de cabra

Peel the eggplants and cut them lengthwise into thin slices. Salt on both sides and lay on paper towels for at least 15 minutes until liquid seeps out. Rinse and pat dry.

Gently fry the eggplant slices in a little olive oil until golden brown, then lay them on paper towels to absorb the excess oil.

Beat the cheese and half & half together until smooth.

Line a deep ovenproof dish or 1lb (450g) loaf pan, about 4 x 5 x 3 inches (9cm x 12cm x 7cm), with plastic wrap, leaving some hanging over the sides. Place a layer of eggplant at the bottom, then a layer of red peppers, and over that spread a layer of creamy cheese. Repeat layers in the same order to fill the dish, ending with a layer of eggplant. Press down firmly, cover with the plastic wrap, and refrigerate for at least 2 hours.

To make the parsley sauce, whiz all the ingredients in a blender or food processor.

To serve, carefully remove the terrine from the dish and cut into slices about ¾in (2cm) thick. Place one slice on each plate, drizzle with the parsley sauce, and garnish with a sprig of mint.

serves 6

3 large eggplants, about 1lb 9oz (700g)

salt, to taste

2 tbsp olive oil

8oz (225g) soft goat's cheese

1½ tbsp half & half

3 red peppers, about 11½ oz (325g), roasted, peeled, seeded, and cut into strips

6 sprigs of fresh mint, to garnish

for the parsley sauce
8 tbsp fresh flat-leaf parsley leaves

3½ fl oz (100ml) olive oil

½ garlic clove, peeled

guacamole
naos guacamole

This very subtle guacamole can be kept chilled in the fridge for a few hours after the first stage of preparation, then finished off just before serving. Have a large bowl of good-quality *taco* chips or warm pita bread to dip into it.

In a bowl, mix together the avocado, Tabasco, lemon juice, olive oil, and orange juice, and salt to taste. Stir in the cucumber, tomato, and shallots.

To serve, sprinkle with *nori* and chives and garnish with radish slices.

3 medium Hass avocados, peeled, pitted, and flesh mashed

dash of Tabasco sauce

2 tbsp each lemon juice and olive oil

2fl oz (50ml) fresh orange juice

salt, to taste

1¾oz (50g) cucumber, peeled, seeded, and diced

1¾oz (50g) tomato, diced

1 shallot, peeled and finely chopped

2–3 sheets *nori* (dried Japanese seaweed), finely shredded

1 tbsp chopped fresh chives

a few radishes, sliced, to garnish

fried squid rings with capers and potatoes
anillos de calamar con alcaparras y perejil

serves 6

Mónica astutely ups the squid ante here by fusing it with wine, punchy garlic, capers, and chili. The end result looks like a homely dish but conceals a sophisticated depth of flavors.

Lightly flour the squid rings and fry them briefly in hot safflower oil, then leave to drain in a colander.

Heat the olive oil in a large frying pan and fry the garlic until just golden. Add the potatoes, crushed chilies, capers, and white wine, and boil until the wine evaporates. Then pour in the chicken stock and bring back to a boil. Season with salt, pepper, and chicken bouillon powder to taste.

Stir in the fried squid rings, lemon juice, and parsley.

Serve in individual bowls, topped with a slice of lemon, a sprig of parsley, and a fried *arbol* chili.

1lb 10oz (750g) fresh squid rings

6oz (175g) all-purpose flour

2 tbsp safflower oil

2 tbsp olive oil

5 garlic cloves, peeled and thinly sliced

12oz (350g) Cambray or small new potatoes, peeled, boiled, and halved

6 *arbol* chilies, crushed

4oz (115g) small capers

10fl oz (300ml) white wine

1¼ pints (700ml) chicken stock

salt, pepper, chicken bouillon powder

juice of 2 lemons

1 tbsp chopped fresh parsley leaves

1 lemon, cut into 6 slices, to garnish

6 sprigs of fresh parsley, to garnish

6 *arbol* chilies, fried, to garnish

artichoke and clam soup
suquet de alcachofa con almejas blancas

At Naos this rich, creamy soup, full of subtle flavors, is served as an appetizer, but it could easily become a main course. If fresh artichoke hearts are unavailable, use frozen ones.

Rinse the clams and discard any with open shells which fail to close when they are tapped on the side of the sink.

In a deep saucepan, sauté the garlic in the olive oil until golden, then add the clams, thyme, and white wine. Cover and cook for 3–5 minutes.

Add the artichoke hearts and the fish stock, season with salt, pepper, and chicken boullion powder, then simmer, uncovered, until the liquid has reduced to a quarter of its original volume. Discard any clams with closed shells.

To make the *beurre manié*, mix the butter and flour to a smooth paste and then form into four balls with your fingers.

Add the cream and the *beurre manié* balls to the soup, stirring continuously until well blended and thickened.

Serve hot in bowls, sprinkled with chives.

serves 4

- 2 large garlic cloves, peeled and thinly sliced
- 3 tbsp olive oil
- 2lb 12oz (1.25kg) fresh clams (about 20), shells scrubbed clean
- 8 sprigs of fresh thyme
- 4fl oz (125ml) white wine
- 4 fresh artichoke hearts, about 10½oz (300g), cleaned and cut into eighths
- 1½ pints (850ml) fish stock
- salt and freshly ground black pepper
- ¼ tsp chicken bouillon powder
- 14fl oz (400ml) fresh heavy cream
- 1 tbsp chopped fresh chives

for the beurre manié
- ¾oz (20g) butter, at room temperature
- ¾oz (20g) all-purpose flour

Much of the success of this sweet-sour recipe depends on the mangoes. They should be very juicy and slightly soft but firm enough to retain their shape when cooked. The mango sauce can be prepared about 30 minutes before the ducks are ready. At the same time, steam some basmati rice as a simple complement to the complex flavors.

roast duck with mango sauce
pato doradito con salsa de mango

Peel and cut the mangoes into bite-sized cubes, reserving their juice. Mix the juice with the brandy and marinate the mango in it for about 15 minutes.

Put two tablespoons of water in a large saucepan, add the sugar without stirring, then add the garlic, chili, and ginger.

Strain the mango, reserving the marinade, and add the fruit and red wine vinegar to the sugary water. Cover and warm over low heat until the sugar dissolves. Do not stir.

Heat the white wine, add to the mango mixture, and simmer to reduce the liquid by a third. The mango cubes should retain their shape. Add 8fl oz (250ml) of water and the soy sauce and, if necessary, adjust the sweet-sour flavor with the balsamic vinegar.

Mix the cornstarch into the reserved mango marinade, pour into the mango mixture, and stir around gently. Simmer until the liquid thickens slightly.

Carve the duckling, transfer to individual plates, and pour some hot mango sauce over each portion.

serves 4–6

4½lb (2 x 2kg) ducklings, roasted

for the mango sauce

2 large, slightly green mangoes, about 1lb 9oz (700g)

2 tbsp brandy

3 tbsp superfine sugar

1½ tsp peeled and finely chopped garlic

1 *arbol* chili, finely chopped

1 tbsp peeled and finely chopped fresh ginger root

3 tbsp red wine vinegar

7fl oz (200ml) white wine

1 tbsp soy sauce

1 tbsp balsamic vinegar, or as needed

1 tbsp cornstarch

braised veal ossobuco in wholegrain mustard sauce
ossobuco braseado con salsa de mostaza antigua

Preheat the oven to 350°F/180°C. Season the veal shanks and lightly coat in flour. Heat the oil in a flameproof casserole and fry the veal shanks until lightly browned on both sides. Remove and set aside.

In the same casserole, sauté the carrots, onions, celery, garlic, bay leaves, thyme, and orange peel until golden. Add the wine and sherry and boil to reduce by half, stirring often to free anything sticking to the bottom of the casserole.

Return the veal to the casserole, stir well then cover tightly with aluminum foil. Make a small hole in the center of the foil to allow steam to escape. Transfer the casserole to the oven and cook for 2 hours 15 minutes.

Meanwhile, prepare the mustard sauce. Heat the butter in a frying pan and sauté the onion, garlic, thyme, bay leaves, and pepper until the onion is softened. Add the wine and simmer to reduce until only one tablespoon of liquid remains.

Pour in the beef consommé and reduce again by half.

Stir in the cream and bring just to a boil, then stir in the two types of mustard and salt and boullion powder to taste. Strain and set aside.

To make the carrot garnish, cook the carrots in boiling water until tender. Drain then toss in the butter and chives.

When the veal shanks are cooked, remove them from the oven, lift the meat out of the casserole, and set aside to keep hot.

Strain the liquid from the vegetables into a frying pan and boil until slightly thickened to form a sauce. Set aside.

Arrange a spoonful of carrot garnish in the center of each plate and pour over some mustard sauce. Dip the pieces of veal in the reserved sauce. Arrange one piece on each mound of carrots and sprinkle with chopped chives.

serves 6

6 pieces of veal shank, 2in (5cm) thick

salt and freshly ground black pepper

2 tsp all-purpose flour

2 tbsp vegetable oil

1lb 9oz (700g) carrots, cut into chunks

6 large onions, peeled and roughly chopped

14oz (400g) celery, cut into chunks

1 bulb of garlic, peeled and chopped

6 bay leaves

4 sprigs of fresh thyme

peel of 1 orange, cut into thin strips

1 pint (600ml) each dry white wine and *oloroso* (sweet) sherry

1¾ pints (1 liter) chicken stock

for the mustard sauce

7oz (200g) butter

6 large onions, peeled and thinly sliced

4 garlic cloves, peeled and finely chopped

2 sprigs fresh thyme

2 bay leaves

¾ tsp white pepper

14fl oz (400ml) each dry white wine and good-quality beef consommé

1¾ pints (1 liter) heavy cream

4 tbsp smooth mustard

2 tbsp wholegrain mustard

salt and beef bouillon powder

for the carrot garnish

10½oz (300g) carrots, cut into batons

2oz (55g) butter

small bunch fresh chives, chopped

In Mónica's hands, this classic example of excellent Italian *trattoria* fare becomes a fantastic amalgam of strong flavors and textures. It is delicious accompanied by a creamy potato purée laced with chopped chives or spring onions.

fig tarts with port sauce
tartas de higos con reducción de oporto

Not everyone will want to go the whole distance to complete the professional look of this complex, though sensational, recipe. If you can't get hold of thyme ice cream, sprinkle some chopped fresh thyme over vanilla ice cream instead.

To make the almond frangipani, beat the butter in a mixing bowl until smooth then whisk in the sugar and almonds. Continue to beat vigorously while gradually adding the egg and egg yolk, one at a time. Add the kirsch and almond extract and mix well.

Fold in the flour, then add the crème patissière and stir to blend well.

Place the pastry squares on a baking sheet and spread with a layer of frangipani. Arrange the fig halves on top and sprinkle with the vanilla sugar. Put in the freezer for 30 minutes to 1 hour, but no longer.

Preheat the oven to 400°F/200°C.

To prepare the port sauce, pour the port into a saucepan, add the sugar, and boil until the mixture has reduced by at least a third.

Remove the tarts from the freezer and bake for 15 minutes.

Remove from the oven and serve hot, topped with a scoop of thyme ice cream and a trickle of port sauce. Decorate each plate with a swirl of vanilla custard, another of chocolate sauce, and garnish with a mint leaf.

serves 6

1lb (450g) ready-rolled puff pastry, cut into 4½in (6 x 12cm) squares

2lb 4oz (1kg) fresh juicy figs, halved

6oz (175g) vanilla-flavored sugar

12oz (350g) thyme ice cream

7oz (200ml) thin vanilla custard or best-quality ready-made custard

75ml (2½fl oz) chocolate sauce (optional)

6 fresh mint leaves, to garnish

for the almond frangipani

3 tbsp butter, softened

3 tbsp superfine sugar

3 tbsp ground almonds

1 large egg

1 egg yolk

1 tsp kirsch

⅛ tsp almond extract

1 tsp all-purpose flour

1½oz (40g) crème patissière or best-quality ready-made custard

for the port sauce

1¼ pints (700ml) port

1lb 2oz (500g) superfine sugar

enrique olvera
pujol

He's young, charming, ambitious, and extremely talented. It seems little can stop the meteoric rise of this Mexico City chef who continues to raise the gastronomic bar. Enrique Olvera's career kicked off with the millennium when he opened his first restaurant, Pujol, at the tender age of 24. Since then a cascade of awards has propelled him to the forefront of Mexico's restaurant scene.

Located on a quiet side-street in the ever-popular Polanco district, Pujol is intimate, modern, cool; pure minimalist-chic. The kitchen, however, hums with concentrated activity, its youthful staff seemingly out to prove a quote from Aristotle pinned to a notice board: "We become what we do from day to day so that excellence is not just an act, but a habit."

Enrique's reputation has been forged by his unique reassessment of Mexican classics, preserving flavors and ingredients but preparing and presenting them in a sophisticated, often witty way. And with his American training at the Culinary Institute of New York, he is only too aware of how important marketing can be to a celebrity chef.

Beaming boyishly, Enrique expands on his approach. "Pujol embodies Mexican fine dining of the 21st-century. All the elements and memories are Mexican, even if it doesn't look like that on the plate. The restaurant only seats 60 because my focus is quality, not quantity. I really want to get Pujol into the world's top 100 restaurants. But I also run a hotel restaurant in

Puebla, La Purificadora – that was partly because I didn't want my talented sous-chefs to leave!"

Above Pujol is a large workshop where Enrique and three sous-chefs hold cooking classes and have room to experiment. "We research old techniques," he explains. "Evolution is about finding better ways to do things. We take apart recipes and look at the best way to cook each element. I don't like the word 'deconstruction': what we do is reinterpret. Mexican food has so many fantastic traditions that haven't been played with – just look at the street food!" His excitement buzzes, grounded in canny wisdom.

And the source of this passion? "I've always loved food. When I was a kid I'd refuse to go to certain friends' homes because their mothers didn't cook well. Mine did, though! It wasn't sophisticated but it was full of flavor. But I didn't decide on cooking as a career until later – before that I wanted to be a priest! A turning point came when my father took me to that New York institution, Le Bernardin. That was when I decided I wanted to do fine cuisine." He reflects for a minute before adding, "Of course I'm proud of what we've done but there's plenty of room for improvement." You wonder just how much further he can go.

zucchini flower cappuccino
cappuccino de flor de calabaza

This amusing variation on a well-known theme is an easy to prepare appetizer that slips down beautifully. Serve it in a glass coffee cup or a simple glass bowl to show off the contents.

Heat the olive oil in a saucepan and sauté the onion and garlic until softened. Tip in the zucchini flowers or spinach and cook until wilted. Then add the *epazote*, milk, and cream and simmer gently for 20 minutes. Salt to taste and blitz in a blender or food processor until smooth. Strain and set aside.

To prepare the coconut foam, heat the coconut milk in a saucepan until it begins to boil. Remove from the heat and beat vigorously with a hand whisk until a foam forms, then allow to settle.

To serve, pour the hot "cappuccino" into cups and spoon some coconut foam on top, using a slotted spoon. Sprinkle with a little grated nutmeg.

serves 4

1 tbsp olive oil

1 small onion, peeled and sliced

1 garlic clove, peeled and sliced

1lb 10oz (750g) zucchini flowers or baby spinach leaves, rinsed

5 leaves fresh *epazote* or flat-leaf parsley

1 pint (600ml) milk

18fl oz (500ml) whipping cream

salt, to taste

freshly grated nutmeg

for the coconut foam
9fl oz (250ml) coconut milk

marinated tuna and sea bass *tostadas*
tostada de atún y robalo semisarandeado

To imitate Enrique's *cocina* is to set off on a voyage of discovery. Each component of the dish needs painstaking preparation and is then assembled on the plate at the last minute. This recipe is an ironic take on a street-food *tostada* (a crisp-fried small *tortilla* with assorted toppings). The fish is virtually sashimi-like, so needs to be absolutely fresh. The result is a work of art, full of color and texture.

Cut the tuna and sea bass into bite-sized pieces, cover with plastic wrap, and refrigerate.

To prepare the marinade, heat the vegetable oil in a frying pan and sauté the onion and garlic until starting to turn golden, then add the *guajillo* chilies, and cook until just golden.

Add the chopped tomatoes and simmer until the mixture thickens. Season to taste. Whiz in a blender or food processor, strain and set aside to cool.

To make the tortilla crumbs, toast the tortillas in the oven until golden and dry, then whiz in a blender or food processor. Set aside until needed.

Put all the ingredients for the avocado purée in a food processor and blend until smooth. Refrigerate until ready to use.

Season the fish pieces and stir them into the marinade. Stir in the lemon juice, chives, and onion strips.

Sprinkle a large ring of *tortilla* crumbs in the bottom of four soup bowls. Place a spoonful or two of the fish mixture inside the ring. Garnish the fish with two cherry tomatoes, a fried chili, and a drizzle of olive oil. Outside the ring place a spoonful of avocado purée and an avocado roll. Serve immediately.

serves 4

5oz (140g) fresh tuna

5oz (140g) fresh sea bass filets

salt and freshly ground black pepper

2 tbsp fresh lemon juice

2 tsp chopped fresh chives

½ red onion, peeled and cut into strips

8 yellow cherry tomatoes, to garnish

4 *guajillo* chilies, fried, to garnish

1–2 tbsp olive oil, for drizzling

1 avocado, peeled, pitted, cut into thin slices, and rolled up just before serving

for the Sarandeado marinade

1 tbsp vegetable oil

1 small onion, peeled and chopped

2 garlic cloves, peeled

3 *guajillo* chilies

1lb 2oz (500g) tomatoes, roughly chopped

salt and freshly ground black pepper

for the tortilla crumbs

8 soft corn *tortillas*

for the avocado purée

2 Hass avocados, peeled, pitted, and cut into chunks

1 tsp vegetable oil

1 tsp fresh lemon juice

salt, to taste

shrimp-filled avocado ravioli
raviol de aguacate relleno

Delicate but with a strong kick from the chili mayonnaise, these avocado "sandwiches" are fantastic. The contrast between the smooth oiliness of the avocado and the crumbly filling is pure heaven!

Melt the butter in a saucepan and sauté the onion and garlic until softened. Add the shrimp and quickly sauté to seal the juices, then cover and cook over low heat for about 7 minutes. Drain, reserving the liquid. Once the shrimp have cooled, briefly mince them in a food processor or blender, and set aside in a bowl.

Boil the potato and carrot in a little water until just tender. Drain, allow to cool, and mix with the shrimp. Stir in the cilantro, the chili, and enough of the reserved shrimp juices to moisten without becoming sloppy. Add salt to taste and set aside.

To make the mayonnaise, blend together the oil, egg yolk, lemon juice, mustard, and salt in a food processor – alternatively use about 7fl oz (200ml) of a good-quality store bought mayonnaise – then stir in the *chipotle* chili pulp. Set aside in the refrigerator.

To make the green oil, quickly blanch the cilantro in salted boiling water, then plunge into iced water to cool. Drain. Put into a blender or food processor with the oil and salt and whiz until intensely green and very smooth.

Just before serving, cut the avocados in half, remove the pits, and slice thinly lengthwise. Place three slices side by side on each serving plate, then put a spoonful of shrimp filling on each slice. Cover with three more slices of avocado.

Top each "ravioli" with a dollop of spicy mayonnaise and garnish with some onion strips and a scattering of lemon zest. Finish with a swirl of green oil, a sprinkling of *fleur de sel,* and a twist of freshly ground pepper.

serves 4

2½ tbsp butter

1 small onion, peeled and finely diced

1 garlic clove, peeled and crushed

2lb 4oz (1 kg) shrimp (about 21–25), cleaned and cut into thirds

1 small potato, peeled and diced

1 small carrot, peeled and diced

small bunch fresh cilantro, chopped

1 *serrano* chili, chopped

salt, to taste

2 large ripe Hass avocados

½ red onion, peeled and cut into strips, to garnish

zest from 2 lemons, chopped, to garnish

fleur de sel or coarse sea salt and freshly ground black pepper

for the chipotle mayonnaise

7fl oz (200ml) vegetable oil

1 egg yolk

1 tsp fresh lemon juice

1 tbsp Dijon mustard

salt, to taste

1oz (25g) *chipotle* chili pulp

for the green oil

small bunch of fresh cilantro

2fl oz (50ml) corn oil

salt, to taste

Tender, slightly pink duck with flourishes of colorful purée, this is another work of art on a plate. Most of the elements can be prepared well in advance so it makes an excellent dinner party dish.

duck breast with three fruit purées
pechuga de pato con tres purés

In a large bowl, mix the soy sauce, sesame oil, ginger, lemon and orange zests, and salt to taste. Add the duck breasts, cover and marinate in the refrigerator for at least 2 hours.

Meanwhile, make the fruit purées. For the apple purée, sauté the apple slices in the butter until tender and golden. Tip into a food processor and blend until smooth. Strain and set aside.

For the date and hibiscus flower purée, cook the hibiscus flowers and dates in plenty of water for about 40 minutes or until the dates are very soft. Drain, leave to cool slightly, then whiz in a blender or food processor until smooth. Strain and set aside.

For the tamarind purée, heat the sugar in a heavy-based saucepan until it caramelizes and turns golden. Take off the heat and very carefully add the tamarind pulp. Stir and simmer over low heat for 20 minutes. Strain and set aside.

For the orange zest confiture, pour 3½fl oz (100ml) of water into a saucepan and add the sugar. Bring to a boil and stir until the sugar is dissolved. Add the orange zest and simmer for 3–5 minutes. Strain and set aside.

Remove the duck breasts from the marinade, pat dry and fry in the oil in a hot frying pan until the skin is golden and the meat is cooked to taste – about 5 minutes on each side for pink, longer for more well done. Allow to sit for 5 minutes before serving.

To serve, smear a spoonful of each purée on one side of the plate and arrange a duck breast on the opposite side. Add a spoonful of orange zest confiture, and garnish with a scattering of thyme leaves and a sprinkling of *fleur de sel*.

serves 4

7fl oz (200ml) soy sauce

4 tsp sesame oil

1 small piece fresh ginger root, peeled and finely chopped

zest of 1 lemon, roughly chopped

zest of 1 orange, roughly chopped

4 duck breasts, with skin on

salt, to taste

2 tbsp vegetable oil

fresh thyme leaves, to garnish

fleur de sel or coarse sea salt, to garnish

for the apple purée

1lb 2oz (500g) apples, peeled, cored, and thinly sliced

2 tbsp butter

for the date and hibiscus flower purée

7oz (200g) fresh hibiscus flowers, rinsed, or 3½oz (100g) dried hibiscus flowers, soaked

14oz (400g) dates, pitted

for the tamarind purée

7 tbsp superfine sugar

16fl oz (500ml) tamarind pulp

for the orange zest confiture

3½oz (100g) superfine sugar

zest of 1 orange, cut into fine strips

rack of lamb in a chocolate crust
rack de cordero en costra de chocolate

The idea of chocolate with lamb sounds unusual, but is based on a traditional *mole* made to go with poultry. The texture and flavor are out of this world. It is possible to simplify the recipe by skipping the garnishes and *mole*.

To prepare the *frijoles*, simmer the black beans, onion, garlic, and *epazote* in plenty of water over low heat for about 4 hours. Salt to taste, drain, and set aside. (If using canned beans, fry the onion and garlic in a drizzle of vegetable oil until softened. Drain and rinse the beans, tip into a bowl and stir in the onion, garlic, and *epazote*.)

To make the plantain purée, bake the plantain in a preheated oven at 300°F/150°C for 30 minutes then remove from the oven. Peel and blitz with the cream in a blender or food processor until smooth. Set aside.

To make the sweet *mole*, whisk the mole paste into 3½fl oz (100ml) of cold water, then simmer in a saucepan for about 15 minutes. Blitz in a blender or food processor until smooth, strain, and set aside.

To make the green bean garnish, blanch the green beans in lightly salted boiling water, refresh them in iced water, and cut them in half lengthwise.

Melt the clarified butter in a large saucepan, and sauté the green beans with the *frijoles*, the tomato concassé, and the cilantro until heated through. Salt to taste and add more butter if desired.

For the chocolate crust, mix the breadcrumbs and grated chocolate together.

Season the lamb with salt or *fleur de sel*. Coat it in the chocolate crumbs and immediately fry in the clarified butter for 4–5 minutes on each side, or until cooked to taste.

To assemble, place a spoonful of green bean garnish in the center of each plate and top with a dollop of plantain purée. Spoon some *mole* onto the plate. Carve the lamb into cutlets and arrange on the *mole*. Garnish with a drizzle of green oil.

serves 4

1lb 10oz (750g) rack of lamb, divided into 4 equal pieces

fleur de sel or coarse sea salt

3½fl oz (100ml) clarified butter

green oil, to garnish (see page 45)

for the frijoles (beans)

9oz (250g) black beans, soaked overnight, or use canned black beans to save cooking time

1 small onion, peeled and chopped

2 garlic cloves, peeled and crushed

2 sprigs fresh *epazote* or flat-leaf parsley

salt, to taste

for the plantain purée

1lb 2oz (500g) plantain

3½fl oz (100ml) whipping cream

for the sweet mole

8oz (250g) black *mole* paste

for the green bean garnish

3½oz (100g) French green beans

3½fl oz (100ml) clarified butter

1½oz (40g) tomato concassé (pulp), from a skinned, seeded tomato

3 tbsp chopped fresh cilantro

salt, to taste

for the chocolate crust

3½oz (100g) fine breadcrumbs

2½oz (70g) grated dark chocolate

creamy lemon meringue pie with frozen yogurt

pie cremoso de limón verde, merengue y helado de yogurt

This wonderful postmodern dessert makes a perfect finale to dinner at Pujol. It is an ironic take on the classic lemon meringue pie. With Olvera's makeover, all the ingredients are visible in an inside-out way.

Preheat the oven to 300°F/150°C.

Whisk the egg whites until stiff and forming peaks, then slowly add the sugar, whisking continuously. Line a baking tray with non-stick baking parchment and spread the meringue mixture thickly on top. Bake for 2 hours or until crisp. Turn off the oven and leave the meringue to cool in the oven until ready to use. Then break into bite-sized pieces.

In a bowl, beat the condensed milk and lemon juice until well blended and starting to thicken. Add the cream cheese and continue beating to form a smooth, thick cream. Refrigerate until well set.

Put the biscuits in a strong plastic bag and bash with a rolling pin, or blitz them in a food processor, until reduced to fine crumbs.

To serve, create a freestanding "piece of pie" on each plate by arranging a triangular layer of biscuit crumbs as the base. Top with the lemon cream crowned by a few pieces of meringue and a scoop of frozen yogurt. Finish with a sprinkling of lemon zest.

serves 4

3 egg whites

7oz (200g) superfine sugar

6fl oz (175ml) sweet condensed milk

2fl oz (50ml) fresh lemon juice

7oz (200g) cream cheese

8oz (225g) María biscuits or any plain sweet biscuit, such as digestive or rich tea

9oz (250g) vanilla frozen yogurt

finely grated zest of 1 lemon

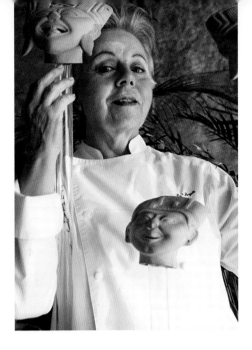

alicia gironella de'angeli
el tajín

"I didn't choose to open a restaurant here – it came to me," says Alicia Gironella dryly, referring to the location of her legendary culinary outpost in Coyoacán, on the southern edge of Mexico City. "I had decided to only write books and teach cookery, but when I was invited to come here, I couldn't refuse." In fact bohemian-chic Coyoacán, with its Aztec past and long intellectual tradition, suits this *éminence grise* of Mexican cooking perfectly. Luminaries such as Frida Kahlo and Leon Trotsky have lived here, and artists and academics still abound.

So it is not surprising that Alicia's restaurant, El Tajín, which was named after a pre-Hispanic site in Veracruz, serves a tantalizing menu of regional specialties. She and her genial Italian husband, Giorgio De'Angeli, co-founder of Mexico's Slow Food movement, both command immense respect. "He's the writer, I'm the cook – though he's good at pasta!" comments Alicia. Since opening her first restaurant in 1993, she has gained a gold medal from France's Académie Culinaire, written the *Larousse Encyclopaedia of Mexican Food* with Giorgio, and even experimented with a Mexican restaurant in India.

Elegant, calm, and collected (it is impossible to imagine even a bead of perspiration on her brow), Alicia is infinitely knowledgeable about Mexican food. This was nurtured by her Yucatecan mother and gourmet Catalan father, a food-importer. Over the years, her expertise and academic approach have mushroomed into a concern for nutritional issues and zealous support of small producers. "Good cooking is about how to use good ingredients. You're responsible for the health of your family – and your clients'," she maintains. The next generation is being inculcated in the background. "I like teaching young people," she comments. "We've developed a university course in the history of Mexico through gastronomy, a kind of culinary anthropology. It's quite fascinating."

Such insatiable intellectual curiosity has steered Alicia's research into pre-Hispanic food. "The indigenous Mexicans were very strong and fit. Their main diet was corn, beans, chilies, squash, and herbs, although each group had its preferred types and cooking methods. Even today each indigenous group has a preferred bean, but the backbone of the diet at every social level is always corn."

Alicia's ongoing crusade is the Mexican diet. "It's changing massively," she continues. "We're seeing disastrous combinations of North American and Mexican foods. These are anathema to our genetic digestive enzymes so obesity is on the rise."

Despite such insights, Alicia's basic motivation is apparent. "Passion for food is not just for yourself, it's about giving other people pleasure." And this she certainly manages.

quelite and ricotta *tacos*
tacos de quelites con requesón

Quelites are wild greens and can be replaced with young spinach or watercress. The blue-corn tortilla adds a strong, rustic flavor. Alicia sourced this recipe in Xochimilco, an area of waterways and floating gardens on the outskirts of Mexico City that is a relic of Aztec days.

Heat the oil in a heavy frying pan. Add the onion, garlic, and chilies and fry gently until softened. Add the *quelites* and the ricotta and season with salt to taste. When the leaves become limp, cover the frying pan with a lid and turn off the heat.

Mix all the ingredients for the *pico de gallo* together and set aside.

Just before serving the *tacos*, drain the liquid that has been released from the *quelites*. Stir in the cilantro and reheat gently.

Heat the *tortillas* quickly on both sides in a non-stick frying pan. Place about two tablespoons of filling in the center of each and roll them up, leaving the ends open.

Serve immediately with the *pico de gallo* or a bowl of hot tomato sauce (see page 52).

serves 4–6

4 tbsp corn oil

1 medium onion, peeled and finely chopped

2 garlic cloves, peeled and finely chopped

2 green chilies, finely chopped

8oz (225g) *quelite* leaves, washed and dried

3½oz (100g) ricotta cheese

salt, to taste

4 tbsp finely chopped fresh cilantro

12 blue-corn *tortillas*

for the pico de gallo (orange and tomato salsa, literally "Rooster's beak")

2 oranges, peeled and segmented, seeds removed

3 tbsp fresh lemon juice

½ onion, peeled and finely chopped

1 tomato, seeded and diced

3 *serrano* chilies, seeded, deveined, and finely diced

3 tbsp extra virgin olive oil

salt, to taste

baked eggplants with apple stuffing
berenjenas rellenas de manzanas

Originally from Sinaloa, in northern Mexico, this makes a great vegetarian main course. It is extremely nutritious, substantial, and full of flavor, especially when served with the hot tomato sauce.

Preheat the oven to 400°F/200°C.

Toss the diced apple in the lemon juice.

Cut the eggplants in half lengthwise. Using a metal spoon, carefully scoop out all but ½in (1cm) of the pulp around the edge, taking care not to break the skin. Finely chop the pulp, mix with the apples, and set aside.

In a large, heavy frying pan, heat the oil and gently fry the onion and garlic until softened, then add the celery, eggplant-apple mixture, and wheat germ.

Cook for 4 minutes, stirring all the time. Stir in the mint leaves, cumin, and nutmeg, then season with salt and pepper to taste. Mix well and remove from the heat.

Grease a baking dish with butter and arrange four eggplant shells in it. Divide the apple mixture between the four shells, then cover with the remaining eggplant halves. Bake for 15–20 minutes or until the eggplant is tender but not too soft.

To make the hot tomato sauce, put all ingredients, except the cilantro, in a saucepan with 2–3 tablespoons of water. Bring to a boil, stirring frequently, and simmer for 10–12 minutes. Remove from the heat and allow to cool a little before blitzing in a blender or food processor. Strain, then stir in the cilantro.

Remove the stuffed eggplants from the oven, sprinkle the cheese over the top, and return to the oven for a few more minutes until the cheese has melted.

Reheat the tomato sauce, pour it into a serving dish, and arrange the stuffed eggplants on top. Serve immediately.

serves 4

4 green apples, about 1lb 5oz (600g), peeled, cored, and diced into ½in (1cm) cubes

2 tbsp fresh lemon juice

4 small eggplants, about 1lb 5oz (600g)

6fl oz (175ml) olive oil

1 small onion, peeled and finely chopped

2 garlic cloves, peeled and crushed

1 celery stalk, leaves removed, thinly sliced

4 tbsp wheat germ

24 fresh mint leaves, chopped

½ tsp cumin

½ tsp nutmeg

salt and freshly ground black pepper

4 tbsp butter

8oz (225g) Cheddar cheese, grated

for the hot tomato sauce

1lb (450g) plum tomatoes, roughly chopped

½ onion, peeled and finely chopped

5 *serrano* chilies, seeded and deveined

salt, to taste

2 tbsp finely chopped fresh cilantro

sweet potato and chicken soup
sopa de camote y pechuga

Sweet potatoes were originally brought to Mexican shores by the Spaniards from West Africa via the Caribbean islands. This particular recipe originated in Querétaro, in the Bajio, north of Mexico City. The soft, sweet pulp combines deliciously with the chicken.

Preheat the oven to 350ºF/180ºC.

Wash and dry the sweet potatoes and place in a baking pan. Cover with aluminum foil and bake for about 30 minutes or until the potatoes are tender when pierced with a pointed knife. Remove from the oven and leave to cool a little, then peel and mash, removing any coarse fibers.

In a food processor, chop up the chicken quite finely. Add the chicken to the sweet potato with the egg yolks, butter, nutmeg, and allspice. Mix well and season with salt to taste. The mixture should have a thick, dumpling-like texture.

Turn the mixture out onto a work surface. Pat out until ½in (1cm) thick and shape into rectangles about 3¼in (8cm) wide, then cut into strips measuring about ¾in x 3¼in (2cm x 8cm).

Bring some water to a boil in a large saucepan, add a little salt, and drop in the strips. Cook for about 20 minutes. Carefully remove the strips from the water with a slotted spoon, drain in a colander, and place in a soup tureen or distribute between individual soup bowls.

Pour the hot chicken stock over the strips and sprinkle with freshly ground black pepper and finely chopped cilantro. Serve immediately.

serves 6

1lb 2oz (500g) sweet potatoes
9oz (250g) skinned chicken breast
2 egg yolks
3 tbsp butter
½ tsp nutmeg
2 allspice berries, ground
3 pints (1.5 liters) hot chicken stock
salt and freshly ground black pepper
3 tbsp finely chopped fresh cilantro

shrimp with tamarind sauce
camarones en salsa de tamarindo

Succulent, sweet, and tart, this fresh-tasting appetizer refreshes the palate before the main course. The combination is delicious, and typical of Gulf Coast cuisine.

Shell the shrimp, leaving the tails on. Save the shells. Remove the black vein along the back of each shrimp, then cut a shallow slit lengthwise down the back and open each shrimp slightly. Season with salt and pepper and brush with half the olive oil. Cover and refrigerate.

In the remaining olive oil, fry the shrimp shells, onion, tamarind pulp, and chilies. Add the stock and simmer for 15 minutes, then remove and discard the shells. Blend the mixture in a food processor and strain through a sieve. Then stir in the sugar or honey. Simmer to reduce so that the sauce thickens slightly and becomes glossy. Season with salt and pepper to taste.

Sauté the shrimp for 2 minutes on each side in a non-stick frying pan, or until pink and cooked through.

To serve, pour some tamarind sauce into the center of each serving plate, and spoon a serving of rice neatly on top. Lay the shrimp around the rice, alternating them with grapefruit segments.

serves 5–6

- 1lb 10oz (750g) jumbo shrimp (at least 25)
- salt and freshly ground black pepper
- 7 tbsp olive oil
- 2 red onions, peeled and chopped
- 1lb 2oz (500g) tamarind pulp
- 2 pickled *chipotle* chilies, very finely chopped
- 18fl oz (500ml) concentrated beef or fish stock
- 4 tbsp light soft brown sugar or honey
- 10½oz (300g) hot, freshly cooked white rice
- 3 large grapefruits, peeled and segmented with seeds removed

crusted roast beef
asado de res con costra

Use top-quality organic beef for this, and serve it with an array of roasted vegetables to create a spectacular centerpiece for a dinner party. It is probably advisable to warn your guests that the crust harbors hidden heat from the chili seeds.

To prepare the marinade, pound the garlic, onion, and peppercorns together in a mortar, then add the oil and vinegar. Blend well to form a paste, adding the herbs for greater flavor.

Rub the marinade all over the beef and place it in a non-metallic dish. Cover with plastic wrap and refrigerate overnight.

To make the crust, mix the rosemary, wheat germ, peanuts, chili seeds, and egg together in a bowl to form a stiff paste. Season with salt and pepper to taste.

Preheat the oven to 400°F/200°C.

Cover the beef with the crust mixture, pressing on firmly so that it stays in place. Put the beef on a rack in a shallow roasting pan and roast for 45 minutes for rare or longer if you prefer it more well done. Remove from the oven and leave to rest for about 8 minutes to let the meat relax and the juices flow.

Pour the stock into a saucepan and strain in the meat juices from the roasting pan. Bring to a boil over high heat and reduce to thicken and form a sauce. Add a little salt if necessary. Pour over the slices of the beef and serve immediately.

serves 6

3lb 5oz (1.5kg) sirloin of beef

9fl oz (250ml) beef or chicken stock

salt, to taste

for the marinade

6 garlic cloves, peeled and crushed

1 small onion, peeled and finely chopped

1½ tbsp whole peppercorns

4 tbsp vegetable oil

2 tbsp white wine vinegar

5 tbsp chopped fresh oregano or rosemary (optional)

for the crust

4 tbsp finely chopped fresh rosemary leaves

2 tbsp wheat germ

3 tbsp finely chopped roasted peanuts

1 tbsp chili seeds

1 egg

salt and freshly ground black pepper

vegetable matchsticks in beef wraps
envueltos de carne con verduras

It is important to use organic beef and bacon for this nutritious recipe. Guacamole and *frijoles refritos* make excellent accompaniments, providing a smooth foil for the crunchy vegetables.

Season the strips of beef with salt and pepper and arrange in stacks of three. Divide the carrot sticks and green beans into six mixed bundles. Wrap a stack of beef strips around one end of each bundle and tie a thin strip of bacon around each roll to secure.

Fry the beef wraps in the oil until lightly browned on all sides and cooked to taste. At the same time, grill or roast the corn under medium heat until tender but crisp.

Melt the butter and stir in the lemon juice, tequila, if desired, and some salt and pepper. Dip the corn halves into the mixture.

Serve on a warm platter, alternating wraps and corn, and drizzle with the remaining butter sauce.

serves 6

1lb 10oz (750g) beef filet, pounded very thin, cut into 18 strips

salt and freshly ground black pepper

3 large carrots, cut lengthwise into sticks and blanched

6oz (175g) green beans, cut in half lengthwise and blanched

2 slices of bacon, each cut into 3 thin strips lengthwise

2 tbsp vegetable oil

3 fresh corn on the cob, cut in half lengthwise

3½oz (100g) butter

2½fl oz (75ml) fresh lemon juice

2 tsp tequila or *mezcal* (optional)

green fig dessert
dulce de higos verdes

As this Yucatecan dessert is extremely sweet, you may want to reduce the sugar slightly. You can also replace the figs with curled strips of papaya. It is perfect after a light lunch, pre-siesta, with cicadas humming in the background.

Boil the figs in water for 8 minutes. Drain and cool. Immerse in the lemon water and set aside.

Put the sugar and 12fl oz (350ml) of water in a large saucepan and heat, stirring continuously, until the sugar dissolves completely. Then boil, without stirring, for about 5 minutes to reach the light syrup stage.

Transfer the figs from the lemon juice to the syrup and add the fig leaf. Simmer for 5 more minutes to thicken the syrup slightly.

Serve the figs in small dishes, doused in syrup, and topped with a dollop of cream.

serves 4–6

12 figs, firm inside but with tender skins

2fl oz (50ml) fresh lemon juice mixed with 2fl oz (50ml) water

13oz (375g) superfine sugar

1 fig leaf

9fl oz (250ml) slightly sweetened whipped cream

strawberries with cheese and honey
fresones con queso y miel

You might need to use toothpicks to hold everything in place, as getting the strawberries to balance on the cheese can be a bit tricky. The red and white stacks still look amazing and taste divine. *Amaranto* seeds are highly nutritious, as long as they are cooked before eating, but may be hard to find outside Mexico and can be omitted.

Arrange the cheese pieces on a flat serving platter and top each with a small piece of fennel, one strawberry, and a trickle of honey.

Sprinkle the entire dish with popped *amaranto* seeds before serving.

serves 4–6

400g (14oz) tangy white cheese, such as Wensleydale or feta, cut or broken into 20 bite-size pieces

4 sprigs fresh fennel

20 large strawberries, cleaned and hulled

9fl oz (250ml) runny honey

8 tbsp *amaranto* (amaranth) seeds, popped like popcorn in a dry frying pan or wok

market food

maría gómez cruz's *esquites*

Anywhere in Mexico City where hungry workers congregate, street food materializes as the good, the bad, but rarely the ugly. At the markets, *pot-au-feu* of tripe or calf's brains simmer gently in huge earthenware *cazuelas* (casseroles): at this high altitude, water boils at a lower temperature so nothing gets overcooked. By late afternoon instant mini-kitchens spit out spirals of smoke on backstreet pavements, braziers glow, and pungent food sizzles. For many *chilangos* (Mexico City residents) this is the gastronomic bottom line: for a handful of pesos, they can eat tasty, mostly nutritious fare while turning a blind eye to hygiene issues, which these days are mainly linked to the storage and freshness of the raw ingredients.

As the light fades and a string of naked light bulbs illuminates the shadows, corn, that sacred Mesoamerican food, takes center stage. Corn-based snacks, *antojítos*, have changed little since Aztec days, with *tortillas* in their multiple incarnations heading the list. A simple variation produces *tostadas*, sometimes called *chalupas* (crisp, quickly fried *tortillas* with a topping of salsa, shredded meat, and sometimes cheese). Soft, warm *tacos* (heated *tortillas* filled with onions, tomatoes, chili, and meat) evolve into *dorados* (fried tacos), *quesadillas* (griddled *tacos* with

cheese), or are rolled into *flautas*. Other typical snacks include *huaraches* (fried oval-shaped *tortillas* with bean paste, chili paste, *nopales* (cactus leaves), and sometimes grated cheese), *elotes* (barbecued or boiled corn on the cob impaled on a stick and sprinkled with chili powder), and mounds of *chicharron* (deep-fried pork skins).

Then there are creamy, crunchy *esquites*. In Colonia Roma, on the corner of Jalapa and Chihuahua, a diminutive figure stands behind a brazier and a rickety table of jars and utensils. María Gómez Cruz is 32, although she looks 19, and when her 15-year-old daughter arrives it is hard to believe they are not sisters – except that María keeps a watchful eye over her two young sons playing in a nearby doorway. By 11pm, María, her children, her cooking equipment, and her juicy *esquites* have vanished without a trace – and you're left wondering whether they were nothing more than a high-altitude mirage.

esquites

serves 4

4 corn on the cobs

2 tbsp corn oil

1 large onion, peeled and finely chopped

salt, to taste

1 tsp dried *epazote* or 1 tbsp finely chopped fresh flat-leaf parsley

4fl oz (125ml) crème fraîche or mayonnaise (or both)

4½oz (125g) crumbly, tangy cheese such as feta, Wensleydale, or Lancashire, finely crumbled

dash of chili sauce

2 tsp chili powder

If possible barbecue the corn; if not, boil until just tender, then slice the grains off the cob and put them in a large bowl.

Heat the oil in a large frying pan and sauté the onion until softened but not browned. Add some salt and the *epazote*, then stir in the corn kernels. Turn the heat down to low, cover and cook for 10 minutes.

Serve in a bowl or cup with a dollop of crème fraîche or mayonnaise, a tablespoonful or so of cheese, and a dash of chili sauce to taste. Finish with a sprinkling of chili powder – though maybe not quite as generous as María would be with it.

"There were chocolate merchants… sellers of kidney beans, sage and other vegetables and herbs, turkeys, rabbits, hares, deer, young ducks, little dogs and other such creatures. Then there were the fruiterers and the women who sold cooked food, flour and honey cake, and tripe… and fisherwomen and the men who sell small cakes…"

A description of the main market in Tenochtitlan (Mexico City), Bernal Díaz, The Conquest of New Spain, *1568*

veracruz

Veracruz! The name immediately conjures up a steamy tropical port packed with carousing sailors, *ceviches,* and the uplifting sounds of the marimba. That certainly exists and the state, also called Veracruz, does curve languidly around the warm waters of the Gulf of Mexico, but the interior paints another, infinitely more varied picture. Lush hills buzz with birds and insects; there are tranquil lakes, trout-filled mountain streams, waterfalls, the *chipichipi* (a persistent mist which keeps things green), and Mexico's highest mountain, the volcanic Pico de Orizaba, cool and snow-capped on the horizon. Such diverse landscapes are matched by a mesmerizing variety of food.

As the doorstep into Mexico for the conquistadors, Veracruz was the point of entry for imported food. Spanish, African, and Caribbean foodstuffs – sugar cane (transformed into local *aguardiente*), rice, peanuts, almonds, pineapples, bananas, citrus fruits, sweet potatoes, and coffee joined indigenous produce such as papaya, mangoes, the melon-like fruit of the *zapote mamey,* vanilla, yucca, and *hoja santa* (a flavorsome herb) to create an inspirational array of ingredients. Put that beside the seafood of the Gulf, from the famed *huachinango* (red snapper) to *róbalo* (sea bass) and succulent *camarones* (shrimp), perfect for portside *ceviches* and *arroz a la tumbada* (seafood rice). Altogether, it is a bountiful land of milk and honey – and you find plenty of that too.

The history of this state is about much more than mere conquest. About 3,000 years ago, the southern half was home to the extraordinary Olmecs, creators of gigantic basalt heads and stone jaguars and thought to have been the first to enjoy the delights of the cocoa bean. Farther north and chronologically later came the Otomies, Huastecs, and the neighboring Totonacs who cultivated the vanilla pod when not practicing flying from poles, something they still indulge in. Fast-forward to 1519, when Hernán Cortés stepped ashore at Villa Rica clutching a cross and followed, unsteadily, by horses laden with trunks of glass beads. His arrival signaled the beginning of *mestizaje* (mixed race) and of culinary cross-fertilization.

The indigenous people kicked off with offerings of "fowls, baked fish, fruit and maize-cakes" together with armfuls of gold, all described in detail by Bernal Díaz. In return, they got the beads and, soon after, pork, beef, spices, and African slaves to cultivate new crops like sugar cane. In this way, Veracruz became the channel through which Old World produce entered the New World of Mexico, as well as seeds from which to grow African and Caribbean foods in the tropical coastal belt. The port maintained a monopoly on this trade until the upheavals of the 19th century, namely a "pastry war" blockade by the French navy, followed by a North American incursion, then occupation by Spanish, British, and French forces, the latter lasting several years. No other region in Mexico has seen such direct foreign input.

Today, although the buzzing port is still vital to the Mexican economy, as is the oil industry farther north in the state, much of the interior is sleepily rural. One exception is the capital, Xalapa (Jalapa), a culturally oriented university town of 400,000 inhabitants. Its culinary claim to fame is the *jalapeño* chili, although this came from being on the transportation route rather than a direct production area. In fact, for centuries Xalapa was the staging post for goods coming from Spain bound for Mexico City, and hosted the country's largest trade fair. Just south of here coffee, tobacco, sugar cane, and dazzling flowers are cultivated in the hills between Coatepec and Cordoba. North of Xalapa lies the epicenter of Mexico's sought-after vanilla crop, which is cultivated in a veritable Garden of Eden around the charming town of Papantla. Still steeped in Totonac traditions, the region also claims the great symbol of this culture, the fabulous archaeological site of El Tajín.

From north to south, its small towns and quaint, colorful villages are characterized by men on horseback, candlelit chapels, tiny *mestiza* women in *rebozos* (shawls) with big shopping-bags hooked over their arms, rusty VW Beetles, and ancient Mustangs. Wood smoke perfumes the night air and dogs, cockerels, and occasionally parakeets perform a stirring dawn chorus. Life is gentle here, seemingly little affected by the outside world.

Typical of such rhythms is the small town of Xico, a mirage of vibrant colors lost in lush banana, sugar-cane, and bamboo-clad hills and surrounded by three volcanoes and a legendary waterfall, the Cascada de Texolo. At full moon, Xico's inhabitants allegedly resort to witchcraft; even the male-run bakery is named Los Brujos (The Sorcerers). There is certainly something special about this town that the conquistadors passed through on their first big march on Tenochtitlan (Mexico City), leaving a legacy of mixed blood and an obsession for good food.

Number one gastro-attraction is *mole de Xico*, darker, sweeter, and richer than the famous Pueblan version thanks to its higher fruit content. Then there are the *toritos* (homemade liqueurs), from *verde*, an emerald green herbal tipple, to peanut and blackberry, all set up for sale on doorsteps. An orange nectar flavors a chicken stew, and two or three others enhance a braised pork dish. Then come the honeys and odd herbs such as *xonéqui*, a small leaf mixed with chilies and eaten with beans. Whether the *brujos* are out or not, what is certain is that with such diverse roots, Veracruz cooking has an incomparable magic.

flor patricia pérez
la fonda
del viejito

Sometimes it is passion, not expense or sophistication, that makes excellent food. This is the case at Xico's La Fonda del Viejito, hidden away down a backstreet of this small, food-obsessed town. The co-owner, Flor (Flower), lives up to her name as she tears off the outer petals from a mass of creamy yucca blossoms. "They're only around in May and June, so we want to make the most of them." She smiles, filling a bowl with the fragrant petals before they are tipped into a bubbling pan. "You can also fry them with onion and tomato to stuff *poblano* chilies, or cook them with garlic, cream, and cheese to fill green or red capsicum peppers."

Although modest in style, with a mandatory TV at one end and plastic tablecloths on the dozen or so tables, La Fonda del Viejito has become a fixture on the Xico eating map, even putting some of the more upscale places in the shade. One reason is the capable, ever-serene Flor Patricia Pérez; another is Pati, her lively kitchen sidekick; a third is a burgeoning new business making *mole* (sauces), salsas, local coffee, and *toritos* (liquers). While channeling their energy into food production, Flor and her husband, Luis Alberto (the *viejito* or old man of their label), have given the restaurant a new lease of life.

Flor grew up in the beautiful colonial town of Cordoba that lies south of Xico over the foothills of the Pico de Orizaba. With the same lushness and climate, the Xico hills give her a fabulous choice of ingredients for recreating dishes from her childhood. "Cordoba was where I first learned about cooking," she relates.

"Then I met my husband and moved to Xalapa where we still live. I went to a cooking school there but I learned local techniques and recipes from two older women, one who's now 86 and still cooks beautifully. A favorite she taught me was a *chileatole*, a broth full of chilies, corn kernels, *masa,* and herbs."

There is nothing complicated about Flor; she tells it as it is, and her life seems to have followed an equally clearly defined path. Every morning, after dropping her two young sons at school in Xalapa, she makes the 30-minute drive to Xico to join Pati, who has already opened the restaurant for breakfast customers. Together they prepare fresh soups and the dish of the day, while turning out *quesadillas* or *huevos rancheros* for ravenous clients. In the corner sits Flor's watchful mother-in-law, a wizened matriarch, often joined by friends who drop by for a chat.

Later, to advance the food production business, Flor takes off to join her husband at a sprawling old house in a neighboring village where production takes shape in a large kitchen opening onto an overgrown garden. "I love traveling through the landscape between the villages," she says dreamily. "It's so green and lush." Such warmth and easy humanity are infectious.

tortilla rolls in tomato sauce
quesadillas entomatadas

serves 4

2lb 4oz (1kg) plum tomatoes

2–3 garlic cloves, peeled

1 medium onion, peeled
and roughly chopped

12 corn *tortillas*

5fl oz (150ml) half & half

4–5 tbsp grated cheese, such
as mature Cheddar

1 *jalapeño* chili, to garnish

Grill or broil the tomatoes, garlic, and half of the chopped onion, turning frequently, for 15–20 minutes until the tomato skins are blackened. Peel away the charred areas then blitz the tomatoes, garlic, and onion in a blender or food processor for a minute or so. Strain the resulting purée through a sieve.

On a hotplate or in a large frying pan, heat the *tortillas* in batches. A minute or so on each side is sufficient, as they must remain soft enough to roll. Alternatively, warm them up in a microwave for 1 minute.

Spoon some of the tomato sauce onto a plate, place a *tortilla* on top, cover it with more sauce, then roll up loosely. Repeat with two more *tortillas*. Drizzle with half & half and sprinkle with the rest of the chopped onion and with the grated cheese. Top with a *jalapeño* chili.

Excellent for lunch or as an appetizer, these *quesadillas* are one of Mexico's infinitely variable dishes. You can add cooked ground beef to make it a more substantial dish and some people like to pop it into a hot oven briefly to melt the cheese. What makes Flor's *quesadillas* extra special is the flavor of the fresh grilled tomatoes in the sauce.

seafood broth
caldo de mariscos

Rumored to cure any sailor's hangover, this soup is pure comfort, packed with tangy flavor and hot chili. The most important stage is the correct preparation of the broth and the *jalapeño* chilies. Use any seafood you wish, but make sure it is absolutely fresh.

Heat the oil in a large saucepan, then add the onion, *jalapeño* chilies, garlic, and tomatoes. Fry over low heat until the onion has softened and the tomato has become a pulp.

Add 1¾ pints (1 liter) of water, the cilantro, bay leaf, and some salt. Cover with a lid and slowly bring to a boil. Carefully drop the seafood and trout into the broth and simmer with the lid on for 10 minutes or until cooked all the way through.

Before serving, remove the bay leaf and add the lime juice.

serves 4

1 tbsp olive oil

1 large onion, peeled and chopped

2 *jalapeño* chilies, seeded, deveined, and sliced, or 2oz (55g) canned *jalapeños* in *escabeche* (pickled chilies)

2 garlic cloves, peeled and crushed

3 medium tomatoes, seeded and chopped

bunch of fresh cilantro, leaves only, finely chopped

1 bay leaf

salt, to taste

14oz (400g) fresh raw shrimp, shelled

10½oz (300g) fresh raw crayfish

1lb 5oz–1lb 9oz (600–700g) trout filet, cut into chunks

juice of 1 lime

This popular fish dish is served all over Mexico but it comes originally from the port of Veracruz. The firm flesh and distinctive flavor of the red snapper work well with the complex, piquant sauce. Match the weight of tomatoes to the weight of your fish. White rice is the classic accompaniment.

veracruz-style red snapper
huachinango a la veracruzana

Make three long diagonal slits on both sides of the fish and place in a non-metallic dish.

In a bowl, mix 5 tablespoons of the olive oil, the lime juice, oregano, marjoram, salt and pepper, then pour over the fish. Cover and leave to marinate in the refrigerator for 2 hours.

In a large saucepan, heat 3 tablespoons of the olive oil and fry the onion and garlic until just softened, then pour in the wine. Simmer to allow the wine to evaporate a little, then add three-quarters of the red peppers, olives, capers, and *jalapeño* chilies, keeping the remainder of each ingredient to use as garnish later.

Cook for 15 minutes then add the tomatoes, *epazote*, fish stock, bay leaves, sugar, and salt and pepper. Stir well and simmer, partly covered, over low heat for 25 minutes.

Preheat the oven to 350°F/180°C. Drizzle 3–4 tablespoons of olive oil over the base of a large ovenproof dish then lay the marinated fish on top. Pour the cooked sauce over the fish and place in the oven. From time to time during cooking, baste the fish with the sauce. After 20 minutes, carefully turn the fish over. Cook for a further 20 minutes or until the flesh is no longer transparent and has cooked all the way through.

Serve immediately, garnished with the remaining red peppers, olives, capers, and chilies. Sprinkle over some freshly chopped parsley or a few sprigs of marjoram.

serves 8

- 2 large red snapper, about 8lb (4kg), scaled and gutted
- 7fl oz (200ml) olive oil
- 4 tbsp fresh lime juice
- ¼ tsp dried oregano
- ¼ tsp dried marjoram
- pinch of salt
- 1 tsp white pepper
- 2 large onions, peeled and finely chopped
- 4 garlic cloves, peeled and crushed
- 7fl oz (200ml) dry white wine
- 8 red peppers, seeded and sliced
- 24 pitted green olives, halved
- 2 tbsp capers
- 10 pickled *jalapeño* chilies, sliced
- 6lb 10oz (3kg) plum tomatoes, roasted, skinned, and seeded
- 2 sprigs of fresh *epazote* or 2 tbsp chopped fresh flat-leaf parsley
- 3–4 tbsp fish stock
- 2 bay leaves
- 1 tbsp superfine sugar
- salt and freshly ground black pepper
- 2 tbsp finely chopped fresh flat-leaf parsley or a few sprigs of fresh marjoram, to garnish

Repeated boiling of the white yucca flowers removes any bitterness. Like spinach, they reduce in volume a lot, so you need to start with masses. They are high in potassium and calcium and popular throughout Central America. Serve with some *frijoles refritos* (refried beans) for a true Veracruzan breakfast. You can also gently scramble the flowers with eggs, tomatoes, chilies, and onion to make *flor de novia* (bride's flower).

In a large saucepan, boil about 1¾ pints (1 liter) water, then add the petals, and leave to simmer for a few minutes before draining. Repeat twice more until the petals become transparent. This should take about 15 minutes in total.

Meanwhile, fry the bacon pieces with a little butter in a large frying pan over medium heat until nearly crisp.

Turn down the heat, add the onion, and sweat until softened. Carefully add the petals, taking care not to break or bruise them. Stir-fry for a few minutes then pour in the eggs and season with salt. Reduce the heat and stir gently to cook the eggs without breaking up the petals. When lightly set, serve immediately.

scrambled eggs with yucca blossom

huevos revueltos con flor de izote

serves 4

10½oz (300g) tender yucca blossoms, outer petals and stems removed

6 slices of bacon, cut into pieces

about 2 tablespoons of butter

1 small onion, peeled and finely chopped

8 large eggs, beaten

salt, to taste

veracruz-style trout
trucha veracruzana

This is Flor's quick-fix trout recipe – a healthy, practical dish that makes full use of an abundance of local river trout. It is a shortened version of the famous Veracruz recipe for *huachinango* (red snapper) on page 76. You could use salmon instead of the trout.

Put all the ingredients, except the trout, in a large saucepan and cook together over low heat for about 8–10 minutes until softened.

Lay the trout filets carefully in the sauce, cover with a lid, and leave to cook gently for 10 minutes or until cooked through. Serve immediately.

serves 2

2oz (55g) pitted green olives, roughly chopped

2oz (55g) capers with their pickling juice

4 medium plum tomatoes, chopped

1 medium onion, peeled and roughly chopped

2 garlic cloves, peeled and crushed

1 tsp dried oregano

1 tsp dried thyme

2 large trout filets

spicy beans
frijoles rancheros

A tasty way to stave off hunger pangs, this dish can be served as an accompaniment with meat or eaten with eggs for breakfast, Mexican-style. Cooking times for beans vary, so just test the softness.

Drain off the soaking water from the beans then tip them into a large saucepan. Cover with cold water, bring to a boil and simmer for at least 2 hours until soft. Drain and set aside.

Heat the oil in a frying pan then add the bacon. As soon as it starts to crisp, tip in the chilies and onion, and fry for another 10–15 minutes. Add the beans and salt. Cook for a few more minutes to heat the beans through. Serve piping hot, sprinkled with grated cheese.

serves 4

1lb 2oz (500g) pinto beans, soaked overnight or for at least 10 hours

1 tbsp vegetable oil

3½oz (100g) bacon, cut into pieces

2–3 *jalapeño* chilies, sliced lengthwise

1 medium onion, peeled and thinly sliced

salt, to taste

3½oz (100g) cheese, such as Parmesan or mature Cheddar, grated

sweet potato and pineapple purée
dulce de camote con piña

Typical of the cosmopolitan style in Veracruz, this sweet mash brings together sweet potato, originally from Africa, and pineapple, which the Spanish introduced from the Caribbean. It is delicious served with a dollop of crème fraîche.

In a large saucepan, cover the sweet potatoes with cold water and bring to a boil. When the water is bubbling, add the sugar and pineapple pieces and boil fast for 15–20 minutes, uncovered, or until the potatoes are soft and the liquid has partly reduced.

Strain and reserve the sweet cooking liquid. Give the pineapple and sweet potato a quick whiz in a blender or food processor, adding just enough of the cooking liquid to produce a smooth mash.

Serve warm or chilled in individual glasses with a spoonful of crème fraîche and a few pineapple chunks.

serves 6

2lb 4oz (1kg) sweet potatoes, peeled, rinsed, and roughly chopped

10½oz (300g) light soft brown sugar

4 thick slices of fresh pineapple, skin and core removed, roughly chopped (keeping some pieces back to garnish)

6 tbsp crème fraîche (optional)

vanilla cream
natilla con vanilla

During Easter week this dessert appears on every table in Mexico, though Flor makes it throughout the year. Mexicans have a very sweet tooth, so you may want to reduce the sugar.

In a saucepan, heat the milk, vanilla pod, vanilla extract, and sugar very gently until just tepid.

Stir in the cornstarch paste and keep stirring over low heat as the mixture thickens until it comes to a boil.

Cool slightly before pouring into individual glass dishes. Chill in the refrigerator.

Scatter over some raisins before serving.

serves 6–8

1¾ pints (1 liter) whole milk

1 vanilla pod, sliced lengthwise with seeds left in

2 tbsp good-quality vanilla extract

7–9oz (200–250g) muscovado sugar

3oz (85g) cornstarch mixed with 4 tbsp of cold water

2oz (55g) seedless raisins

market food

doña juanita's *mole*

There is a sense of a 1950s children's story in the kitchen of Doña Juanita Montenera Básquez. Rows of turquoise enamel saucepans and miniature pottery *cazuelas* (casseroles) hang against a flowery plastic wall cloth, while a back door frames a tiny garden bursting with color. Though modest, the room is neat and scrubbed clean, and cheerful chatter comes from her three nieces seated around the kitchen table.

Doña Juanita herself, tiny, slender, and bright-eyed with her snowy-white hair pulled back in a single braid, stands erect, smoothing down her checked pinafore. She epitomizes the kind old lady who sells homemade ice creams to school kids for a few pesos, then pats them on the head and drops the coins into a tin on top of the fridge. The unusual flavors of her colorful ices – carrot, peanut, coconut, strawberry, and blackberry – are all part of the fairytale image.

Now in her late 70s, Juanita's life begins and ends in Xico, although she did spend 15 years in Mexico City working as a nanny. Today, her sense of "foreign" means someone from Coatepec, the coffee-growing town down the hill, or from Xalapa, half an hour's drive away.

Juanita may have a heart of gold but she is also astute. In Xico, *mole* is a burgeoning cottage industry but for quality Juanita's beats all rivals, enabling her to sell it at above the market rate. She cannot remember when she first started making *mole* but now keeps to a monthly schedule of cooking 66lb (30kg) batches. "It takes one day to prepare the ingredients and another day to cook them," she explains. "Someone comes to help with the stirring as I'm not strong enough nowadays." She takes a jarful out of the fridge. "You can also have it for breakfast, you know, on a *tortilla* with a bit of cheese and onion," she says helpfully. Given how delicious it is, that sounds like an excellent idea.

mole de xico

This makes a large quantity but keeps in the fridge for weeks. The rich, fruity sauce should be poured over cooked meat, but avoid eating it in the evening as it is hard to digest. There are no fixed rules to making *mole,* quantities can be altered to give different accents. Play with the combinations and proportions.

Rinse the chilies with cold water, pat dry with a paper towel, then grill on a hot griddle or place under a broiler. Turn frequently to ensure an even charring. Split and seed the chilies while they are still warm.

Heat the oil in a thick-bottomed saucepan and fry the chilies in batches until dark. Tip the chilies into a bowl, leaving the oil in the saucepan, and cover them with boiling water. Set aside.

Toast the pumpkin seeds and almonds until golden, and dry-fry the sesame seeds. Put all the nuts in a food processor and grind to a fine, buttery-smooth consistency. Set aside.

Blend the onion, garlic, bread, and *tortilla* in a food processor. Add the plantain, prunes, raisins, aniseed, and cloves and continue processing until well combined.

Gradually whiz the chilies into the mixture, little by little to make sure they are evenly distributed. Add a little of the chili soaking water to loosen. Add the ground nuts and cinnamon and blend the mixture to form a rich, smooth paste.

Reheat the reserved oil in the saucepan and, when hot, carefully spoon in the paste and stir well. Bring to a boil, add the sugars, mix well, and lower the heat. Simmer gently over low heat for 20–25 minutes, stirring continuously to avoid burning.

Pour in the stock, a little at a time, stirring all the time until completely incorporated. When the mixture comes to a boil, stir in the chocolate until it has melted and is thoroughly blended.

Cover the saucepan and simmer over low heat, stirring frequently, for 1–1½ hours. The *mole* should develop a thick, creamy consistency. Set aside to cool. Then transfer to sterilized jars, seal, and keep in the refrigerator until required.

makes 3½ pints (2 liters)

- 9oz (250g) *mulato* chilies
- 2oz (55g) *pasilla* chilies
- 2oz (55g) *ancho* chilies
- 4fl oz (125ml) sunflower oil
- 1oz (25g) toasted pumpkin seeds
- 1oz (25g) blanched almonds
- 1oz (25g) sesame seeds
- 1oz (25g) peanuts, skinned
- 1oz (25g) shelled walnuts, soaked in milk overnight and skinned
- 1oz (25g) pine nuts
- 1oz (25g) hazelnuts
- 1 large onion, peeled and finely chopped
- 3 garlic cloves, peeled and finely chopped
- 1 slice dry or toasted white bread, crumbled
- 1 fried corn *tortilla,* crumbled
- 1 large ripe plantain, peeled (soak in warm water for 15 minutes to aid peeling) and sliced
- 2oz (55g) prunes
- 2oz (55g) seedless raisins
- 1 tsp aniseed
- 3 cloves
- 1 tsp cinnamon
- 1oz (25g) muscovado sugar
- 1 tbsp granulated sugar
- 2½ pints (1.5 liters) chicken, turkey, or vegetable stock
- 3½oz (100g) dark chocolate (70% cocoa), broken into pieces

puebla

Think Puebla, think *mole*, as this city is the original source of that almost mythical dark sauce. Somehow it seems fitting, as the extraordinarily eclectic ingredients (*mole* comes from the Nahautl word *molli*, meaning "mixture") perfectly match the baroque facades of the city itself. Deeply traditional, fervently Catholic, and with a strong Spanish character, Puebla, Mexico's fourth largest city, just missed becoming the capital when it was founded in 1531. The area was already a thriving pottery center due to abundant local clay, but this was transformed when the Spaniards brought new techniques of tin-glazed ceramic, a type of highly decorative majolica, from the Castilian town of Talavera. With the flood of friars and nuns who came to fill the monasteries and convents, the stage was set for Puebla's foodie status.

Puebla state borders verdant Veracruz to the east and the arid sierra of Oaxaca to the south. It is topographically very different from its neighbors, as it sits on the high central plateau of Mexico with a correspondingly temperate climate. Westwards, Mexico City is a short hop away; such proximity contributes to a dynamic and modern industrial economy, which keeps the restaurants on their toes and gives the city a busy commercial air. Puebla is also located in the shadow of Mexico's famous volcanoes, snow-capped Popocatépetl and Iztaccíhuatl, with La Malinche to the north; their potentially threatening silhouettes loom over ploughed fields and industrial oases, reflections of the state's slightly schizophrenic nature.

In prosperous downtown Puebla, where huge fortunes have been made in the textile industry, mansions are inlaid with tiles, occasionally rendered in vivid colors and adorned with ornate stuccowork and wrought-iron balconies. Around them the bells of hundreds of churches toll incessantly. The peals are a constant reminder of the thousands of nuns, usually daughters of the Creole elite, who, from the 17th century onwards, taught indigenous converts Spanish cooking techniques, such as frying and roasting. Even today the buttery cakes sold at the doors of the convents have nothing of Mexico about them: no chili, no *epazote*!

The nuns certainly cooked in splendor, as witnessed by the Talavera tiling in the kitchen of the former Convent of Santa Monica. Though a decorative masterpiece, this extravaganza cannot hold a candle to the breathtaking Capilla del Rosario inside the church of Santo Domingo a few blocks away. The carving is prodigious, beautiful, a riot of gold leaf and intricacy, blinding in its workmanship. In the pews, women sit silently, heads bowed, eyes closed, lips moving in fervent prayer, while at the gate a blind trumpeter blasts a serenade.

A sweet-toothed enclave lies just east of here in Calle 6 Oriente, a street entirely dedicated to the sale of sweets, biscuits, and candied fruit. Ubiquitous and unique to Puebla is the *camote*, or candied sweet potato. Simply cooked with sugar and lemon or orange extract, the handrolled, individually wrapped *camotes* grace every shop window, where they are joined by brilliantly colored and wrapped fruit jellies, crystallized fruits, *dulces de Santa Clara*, cakes, and jars of fudge syrup. Of course plenty of young Pueblan noses are pressed against the glass. Adults are more interested in bottles of *rompope*, a sweet eggnog packed with rum, almonds, and cinnamon. Surprisingly, this too is said to have been invented by nuns, maybe on a bad-cake day.

Pueblan traditions often seem etched in stone, as just two historical dishes dominate the city's cuisine: *mole poblano* and *chiles en nogada* (see pages 92 and 95). Pueblans revel in relating the origins of the famous sauce: the most credible version attributes its creation to a nun at the convent of Santa Rosa, with or without divine intervention. Legend has it that, desperate to impress a visiting bishop and disguise a rather skinny turkey, she panicked and threw half the contents of the store-cupboard into a mortar and started grinding, then emptied the other half – including chocolate – into a huge *cazuela*. Several hours of stirring later, *mole poblano*, in all its unctuous, 30-odd ingredient splendor, was born. Another very plausible theory is that it was derived from a traditional indigenous sauce for turkey that even Moctezuma enjoyed. In the convent, this was refined with Asian spices brought by the Spaniards and had the chocolate added, an ambrosia hitherto reserved by the Aztecs only for drinking – by men alone.

Chiles en nogada (stuffed *poblano* chilies in walnut sauce with pomegranate seeds), on the other hand, is heavily symbolic as its red, green, and white colors reflect the Mexican flag. This recipe is said to have evolved in the convent of Santa Monica (or possibly Santa Rosa) to celebrate Independence in 1821. It was originally only made in August and September, the walnut and pomegranate season: perfect timing for the patriotic dish to be served every subsequent Independence Day on September 16. Thanks to the elevated status of this dish and the ubiquity of *mole poblano*, Puebla can claim the consolation of being top notch in the annals of Mexican gastronomy, even if it failed to become the capital city.

alonso hernández
mesón de la sacristía

Justifiably proud of their cuisine, the people of Puebla also insist that it is the true cuisine of Mexico. Every taxi driver will tell you this. Non-Pueblans declare that this is based purely on the legendary chocolate-based *mole*, invented in a Pueblan convent. Alonso Hernández, the young chef at the Mesón de la Sacristía, begs to differ and jumps at the chance to expand on the subject.

"Puebla is definitely the crossroads of Mexican food. All roads come here from the coast of Jalisco in the west to Veracruz in the east. You could call our cooking the first fusion food, as it a mix of French, Spanish, and Arab influences. In fact, Puebla was founded as the capital of Mexico, before Mexico City. The Spaniards brought monks and, soon after, nuns and they cooked the most sublime food. When the indigenous people converted to Catholicism, they were forced to change their way of eating and cooking. Butter, for example, was unknown to them. Some of the best cakes and *mole poblano* are still made by the nuns. But," he adds, with a tinge of regret, "unfortunately they won't reveal their recipes."

Although hailing from Mexico City, Alonso recounts Pueblan gastronomic history with as much sustained enthusiasm as he puts into his cooking and teaching. Food was not always his chosen career, however. "I started off studying chemical engineering at university, then realized how much I liked mixing substances and the whole alchemical process. So I became a chef. Later I did a postgraduate degree in gastronomy. A friend of mine did a doctorate on 'the lemon': nothing less, nothing

more. It's fascinating to focus on one element like that." With such a background, Alonso's love of theorizing comes as no surprise.

"We Mexicans really recognize the value of food. A few years ago there was a proposal to give all Mexican cooking UNESCO World Heritage status. It didn't happen, but they're trying again and it may well work. Young chefs like myself are backing it by cooking increasingly with local, unprocessed ingredients.

"I only use the three basic techniques of roasting, boiling, and frying but I am also careful about ingredients," Alonso continues. "I never use olive oil, for example, as that's not Mexican. I stick to corn, vegetable, or peanut oil. I've discovered new things on my travels to places like Oaxaca, Chiapas, and Cancun."

Alonso's methodical approach is appreciated by his employer, Leobardo Espinosa, the young son of an old Pueblan family. "We've had top chefs from Boston and New York attending Alonso's classes," says Leobardo with obvious satisfaction. "We really want to show people the riches of Puebla." That sense of Pueblan greatness will just not go away.

Tomatillos have a tart flavor which makes them an invaluable ingredient. The main flavor of this simplified *mole* comes from the strong, smoky *chipotle* chili, which is in fact a dried and smoked *jalapeño* chili with a lingering heat – some would say burn. It is delicious with organic chicken, pork, or even grilled fish.

smoky sacristía *mole*
mole sacristía

Grill the *tomatillos*, onion, and garlic on a hot griddle or under a broiler, turning frequently to brown on all sides.

Fry the *chipotle* chilies in the oil until they turn golden brown.

Blend the tomato, onion, garlic, and chilies together in a blender or food processor with a little water to form a smooth purée. Pour the purée into a saucepan and simmer over low heat for 10 minutes. Add enough chicken stock to form a thick sauce, heat through, and season with salt.

serves 4–5

1lb 2oz (500g) *tomatillos,* fresh or canned

2 onions, peeled and roughly chopped

1 garlic clove, peeled

3 *chipotle* chilies

1 tbsp vegetable oil

9fl oz (250ml) chicken stock

salt, to taste

traditional *mole poblano*
mole poblano

Heat 2in (5cm) vegetable oil in a deep saucepan. When hot, fry the chilies until crisp. Remove and lay on paper towels to absorb the excess oil. Save the oil.

Grill the tomatoes, onion, and garlic on a hot griddle or under a broiler, turning frequently to brown on all sides.

Put the chilies and grilled tomatoes, onion, and garlic in a large saucepan and pour in 1¾ pints (1 liter) of water. Bring to a boil, then reduce the heat and simmer for about 10 minutes or until the chilies are soft.

Blend the vegetables and cooking liquid together in a food processor to make a sauce. Strain and set aside.

Fry the plantain in the reserved oil until lightly browned.

Toast the *tortilla* on both sides under a broiler until completely blackened.

Blend the plantain and *tortilla* together with 2½ pints (1.5 liters) of water in a food processor. Strain to form a smooth sauce and set aside.

Bring the chili sauce to a boil in a saucepan and cook for about 10 minutes. Then stir in the plantain sauce and the chicken stock. Add the chocolate and sugar, bring to a boil and simmer for 45 minutes.

serves 4–5

vegetable oil

3 *mulato* chilies, stems and seeds removed

3 *ancho* chilies, stems and seeds removed

3 *pasilla* chilies, stems and seeds removed

1lb 2oz (500g) tomatoes

7oz (200g) peeled and roughly chopped onion

2 garlic cloves, peeled

1 plantain, peeled (soak in warm water for 15 minutes to aid peeling) and chopped

1 corn *tortilla*

8fl oz (225ml) chicken stock

3¼ oz (90g) dark chocolate (70% cocoa), broken into small pieces

3½ oz (100g) dark soft brown sugar

Dried *mulato, ancho,* and *pasilla* chilies are all available by mail order. *Mulato* and *ancho* chilies are similar in flavor, except that the *mulato* is slightly sweeter, while the *pasilla* is much punchier. Although far from having the legendary 20–30 ingredients, Alonso's *mole poblano* tastes like the real McCoy. Serve it with any meat or vegetable of your choice.

green pumpkin seed sauce
pipián verde

This sumptuous green sauce can be served with poultry or with pork. Sauces thickened with pumpkin seeds were used extensively by the Mayas and later the Aztecs.

Grill the *tomatillos*, onion, garlic, and chilies on a griddle or under a broiler, turning frequently to brown on all sides.

Put the grilled *tomatillos*, onion, garlic, and chilies in a blender or food processor and add the cilantro, *epazote*, and 9fl oz (250ml) of water. Whizz until well blended and set aside.

Fry the pumpkin seeds in the oil until golden, then reduce to crumbs in a coffee grinder. Mix the crumbs with 9fl oz (250ml) of water and cook in a saucepan over a medium heat for 2 minutes.

Put the pumpkin seed mixture and chili sauce into a saucepan and mix together. Bring to a boil, add the chicken stock, season with salt and simmer, uncovered, for about 15 minutes until thickened.

serves 4–5

1lb 2oz (500g) *tomatillos*, **fresh or canned**

3 large onions, peeled and halved

2 garlic cloves, peeled

1½oz (40g) *serrano* **or** *jalapeño* **chilies, seeded, deveined, and roughly chopped**

bunch of fresh cilantro, leaves only

bunch of fresh *epazote* **(optional)**

8oz (225g) hulled pumpkin seeds

1 tbsp vegetable oil

9fl oz (250ml) chicken stock

salt, to taste

cream of bean soup
crema de frijol

Black beans are quintessentially Mexican, particularly popular among the Mayas. Serve the soup garnished with fried *chipotle* chilis and cubes of fresh goat's cheese.

Drain the soaked beans and place them in a large saucepan. Add enough water to cover them and add the onion.

Bring to a boil, reduce the heat, and simmer slowly for about 2 hours, or until the beans are softened. Whiz the beans with their cooking liquid in a blender.

Heat the oil in a large saucepan and fry the chopped onion until golden. Add the bean mixture, bring to a boil and add 1¾ pints (1 liter) of water and salt to taste. Simmer for 3 minutes until heated through.

serves 4–6

1lb (450g) black beans, soaked in water overnight

1 small onion, peeled and quartered

salt, to taste

3 tbsp vegetable oil

1 small onion, finely chopped

stuffed chilies in walnut sauce
chiles en nogada

Alonso's recipe for Puebla's famous classic is packed with fruit which, when combined with the rich cream sauce, makes a truly substantial dish. If you cannot find *poblano* chilies, substitute pointy green bell peppers.

To make the stuffing, heat 1 tablespoon of the oil in a large frying pan and sauté the onion and garlic for about 5 minutes or until the onions are transparent. Add the tomatoes and fruits, then stir in the sugar. Cover and simmer gently for 20 minutes.

Meanwhile, in a large saucepan, heat the remaining oil, tip in the beef and pork, and add a pinch of salt. Stir continuously until evenly browned. Then pour in the fruit mix and stir in the almonds and raisins. Simmer, uncovered, for 10 more minutes to thicken slightly. Set aside.

To prepare the walnut sauce, blend the cheese, milk, sugar, sherry, and the walnuts in a food processor to form a thick, sweet cream.

Grill the *poblano* chilies on a hot griddle or under a broiler until they are slightly charred but not soft or overcooked. Place in a plastic bag to sweat for 15 minutes then peel off the charred skin under cold running water. Slit the chilies carefully down one side, remove the seeds and veins, and pat the outside dry. Stuff with the meat and fruit mixture, and set aside.

Beat the egg yolks and reserve. Whisk the whites with the salt until stiff and holding peaks. Gently fold in half the reserved yolks and a pinch of flour, taking care to prevent the foam from collapsing and becoming liquid again.

Lightly coat the stuffed chilies in flour, then dip in the egg mixture, turning to cover evenly. Pour ¾–1¼in (2–3cm) of oil into a large, deep saucepan and warm over high heat. When hot, lower the heat to medium and gently add one chili at a time into the oil. Fry for 2–3 minutes, carefully spooning hot oil over the chili, until the batter is crisp. When cooked, remove each chili and lay on paper towels to absorb the excess oil.

Serve warm, bathed in the cream sauce and with a scattering of pomegranate seeds and chopped parsley.

serves 6

6 large *poblano* chilies

3 large eggs, separated

¼ tsp salt

3¼oz (100g) all-purpose flour

1½ pints (850ml) vegetable oil

seeds from 1 pomegranate, to garnish

bunch fresh flat-leaf parsley, chopped, to garnish

for the stuffing

2 tbsp sunflower oil

1 onion, peeled and chopped

1 garlic clove, peeled and crushed

1lb 10oz (750g) tomatoes, diced

2 apples, peeled, cored, and diced

1 pear, peeled, cored, and diced

2 ripe peaches, peeled, pitted, and diced

1 tbsp granulated sugar

8oz (225g) ground beef

8oz (225g) ground pork

pinch of salt

1¾oz (50g) flaked almonds

1¾oz (50g) seedless raisins, soaked to soften, and drained

for the walnut sauce

7oz (200g) ricotta or cream cheese

9fl oz (250ml) milk or sour cream

2oz (55g) granulated sugar

1 tbsp sherry

1lb 2oz (500g) shelled walnuts, soaked in milk overnight and skinned

fried parsley with shrimp
perejil frito

The parsley in this appetizer contrasts splendidly with the juicy shrimp, sharp lime, and smoky flavor of the cream cheese.

Rinse the parsley, remove the stems, and pat dry. Fry in the hot oil over high heat until golden. Remove from the oil, lay on paper towels to absorb the excess oil, and set aside.

Fry the bacon in the same oil until just crisp. Remove from the pan and lay on paper towels to absorb the excess oil.

To make the cream cheese dressing, mix all the ingredients together.

To serve, arrange the parsley on a serving plate, top with the shrimp and bacon, and drizzle with lime juice. Season with salt to taste and serve with the cream cheese dressing.

serves 4

2 large bunches fresh flat-leaf parsley
1 pint (600ml) vegetable oil
7oz (200g) Canadian bacon, diced
3oz (85g) cooked shrimp
juice of 1 lime
salt, to taste

for the cream cheese dressing
4½oz (125g) *chipotle* chili salsa
12oz (350g) cream cheese
dash of soy sauce
dash of Worcestershire sauce

restorative chicken consommé
consommé para un enfermo

Comforting stuff on a cold winter's day, this soup warms the cockles and does not take long to make.

In a large saucepan, simmer the chicken breasts in 3½ pints (2 liters) of water with the onion, garlic, and salt, covered, for 30 minutes or until the chicken is cooked through. Remove the chicken breasts, cool, and shred coarsely.

Strain the stock into a clean saucepan and add the shredded chicken, rice, chilies, and onion. Simmer with the lid on for 10 minutes. Serve immediately, garnished with avocado slices.

serves 6

2 chicken breasts, skinned
1 medium onion, peeled
1 garlic clove, peeled
1 tsp salt
4 tbsp freshly cooked long-grain rice
5 *serrano* chilies, seeded and finely chopped
1 small onion, peeled and finely chopped
bunch of fresh cilantro, chopped
avocado slices, to garnish

tortilla and spicy beef snacks
chalupas

serves 4

8 small corn *tortillas,* about 4 inches
  (10cm) in diameter

vegetable oil

8fl oz (250ml) green chili sauce

8fl oz (250ml) red chili sauce

1 small onion, peeled and finely diced

9oz (250g) shredded cooked beef

Fry the *tortillas,* 1 or 2 at a time, in some oil on both sides until crisp. Without removing them
from the pan, place a tablespoon of chili sauce on top of each one, alternating colors. Top with
some onion and shredded beef.

Serve immediately.

Walk around the corner from *Mesón de la Sacristía* and you may find a stout little lady on a street corner turning out *chalupas* until late at night. Clubbers love them. Typical of Pueblan street food, they make tasty little snacks or appetizers, but should be crisp and freshly made.

market food

las cemitas de las poblanitas

For the average, hungry, low-income Pueblan, nothing beats *cemitas*. A *cemita* is a giant sesame-seed roll thickly spread with avocado and filled with chicken or beef (or in some cases roast kid), *frijoles refritos* (refried beans), *papalo* herbs, Oaxacan cheese, and *chipotle* chili, plus a dollop of salsa. In other words, it is the nutritious Pueblan equivalent of a MacDonalds.

Acknowledged as the best place to find *cemitas,* the market of El Carmen is a few blocks south of the *zócalo* (central square), past Puebla's beautiful tiled facades, a convent or two, a multitude of cheap eateries, and maybe a truck delivering milk-churns. Inside the echoing building, a small market surrounds an altar of extraordinary grandeur, with a glittering though dusty chandelier, several images of the Virgen de Guadalupe (Mexico's much revered patron saint), a brilliant green neon cross, and a massive swathe of theatrically draped curtain. A vase of red gladioli completes the eclectic arrangement.

Equally striking, though on an auditory level, is the sound of rhythmical beating. This emanates from a corner of the building where a dozen or so young women in immaculate white pinafores thump, roll, and beat out dough. This is the kitchen of Las Poblanitas. After making the dough, the girls turn to frying pieces of breaded chicken and beef and chopping avocado. Soon they are assembling hundreds of *cemitas* for the lunchtime rush. It is like a production line in a factory, with large *cazuelas* (casseroles) of ingredients lined up on the counter, the rolls baking in a huge oven, and the sizzle of chicken or beef schnitzel on the stove. Nothing interrupts the girls' concentration, especially when the boss-lady is at the till.

Like its cousin, the English sandwich, the *cemita* has a history, apparently linked to Puebla's 19th-century industrial boom. The *cemita* was the portable lunch *par excellence* for thousands of workers and craftsmen employed by the mushrooming ceramics workshops and textile factories. The origin of the name is shrouded in mystery. One theory is that it derived from the word *semite* that in Moorish Spain identified the unleavened bread made by the Jewish population. Whether true or not, the *cemita* seems unfailing in its function.

These are the perfect picnic rolls – you won't need anything else to eat. *Papalo*, a slightly bitter aromatic herb, grows wild throughout Mexico but is particularly popular in Puebla and neighboring Tlaxcala where it is used in green salsas and guacamole.

filled pueblan rolls
cemitas poblanas

serves 8

8 large crusty sesame rolls
(the Pueblan ones measure
4½ inches (12cm) in
diameter)

4 ripe Hass avocados, peeled,
pitted, and flesh mashed
or sliced

8 tsp mayonnaise (optional)

4 breaded chicken breasts,
halved, fried until cooked
through and kept warm

9oz (250g) *frijoles refritos*
(refried beans)

9oz (250g) white cheese, such
as mozzarella or fresh goat's
cheese, cut into strips

3½oz (100g) *chipotle* chilies,
sliced

a handful of fresh *papalo*
or cilantro leaves

Cut the rolls in half, spread each side generously with avocado and/or mayonnaise. Lay the warm chicken on top of one slice, top with a spoonful of beans, sliced avocado (if not used as a spread), and cheese strips.

Finish with some slices of *chipotle* chili and a few *papalo* leaves and close with the other half of the roll.

michoacán

Land of the redoubtable Purépechas, the only indigenous group to resist the Aztecs, Michoacán is also Mexico's big hunting and fishing state. The Nahuatl name actually means "land of fishermen," a reference to the extensive lakes that nestle between conifer-clad hills on central Mexico's high plateau. Agriculture naturally dominates this fertile land, and cowboys and cattle have high profiles, as do pick-up trucks, avocados (Michoacán is Mexico's main producer), freshwater fish and their saltwater cousins down on the Pacific coast. Matching this array of victuals, a thriving crafts tradition produces high-quality copperware, lacquerware, woodwork, and ceramics, all versatile utensils for preparing and serving a particularly piquant cuisine.

In contrast to the pastoral surroundings, the state capital of Morelia bears a striking colonial imprint. Helped by the indigenous people, whom they dubbed Tarascans, the conquistadors moved in smartly in the 1540s to build this regional capital. There was something about the bounty of the land, its resemblance to northern Spain, and the temperate climate that soon lured a stream of nobility from Spain. An aristocratic air remains in the beautiful arcades surrounding Morelia's main square, the many elegant mansions, the university (actually Mexico's first, though it was transferred here from neighboring Pátzcuaro), and the massive pink-stone cathedral. Along with architecture came Spanish farming and food, but rather than supplant existing dishes, the native diet was enriched by the imported spices, pork, beef, and rice. More than any other city in Mexico, Morelia wears its Spanish heritage proudly. Ironically, it was also the birthplace of José Maria Morelos, one of the main protagonists of Mexican independence who cut the umbilical cord.

Just west of Morelia, along serpentine roads weaving through the hills, lies its complement: Pátzcuaro. This evocative time capsule of cobbled streets and tiled roofs was founded even before Morelia and intended as the hub of self-governing craft communities dotted around the nearby lake. The proto-socialist idea came from Michoacán's enlightened first bishop, Vasco de Quiroga, who was inspired by Thomas More's *Utopia*.

The Purépechas were, and still are, drawn to the shores of Pátzcuaro Lake, partly because of its excellent *pescado blanco*, a delicate little white fish that they catch with butterfly-nets, although its numbers have declined massively due to over-fishing. One lakeside village, Tzintzuntzan, the former Purépecha capital, harbors an agricultural anomaly: a colonial olive-grove in a churchyard. One of Bishop Quiroga's many projects (another was the banana seed, which he brought from the Caribbean island of Santo Domingo), it miraculously escaped a subsequent edict banning olive cultivation due to competition with Spain's domestic industry. Were the trees blessed?

What is certain is that Pátzcuaro is bursting with delicious street food. Few towns can match the variety, quality, and atmosphere of the myriad stallholders who set up their braziers on Plaza Gertrudis Bocanegra from early morning to late at night when wood smoke fills the chilly air. Successive shifts of *rebozo*-draped women cook up *carnitas* (a kind of pork confit), *pollo placero* (chicken, potatoes, carrots, and *enchiladas* in chili sauce), *tacos*, *minguichi* (a cooked, seasoned cheese), *corundas* (pyramid-shaped *tamales* of corn husks filled with chili and creamy corn boiled with wood ash, plus cheese, and/or beef), *uchepos* (another *tamal*, made with sweet, young corn), and *atoles* (thick, soupy corn gruels with flavors such as tamarind). There is even a local tipple, *charanda*, brewed from fermented sugar cane. Daytime treats come in the form of seafood *cocteles* from the coast and, at the market, Michoacán's prodigious wild honeys, cheeses, and pots of thick cream.

With so much dairy farming, it is no surprise that Mexico's largest chain of ice-cream shops bears the name La Michoacana due to the roots of its two founding brothers, who opened their first shop in the 1940s. More venerable still is Pátzcuaro's Nievería La Pacanda, which has been dishing out ice cream since 1905. Throughout the state, the most common flavor is *de pasta*, sweet and creamy with touches of cinnamon, honey, and almonds, but La Pacanda heads out into quirkier zones of pine nut, cheese, tequila, fig, peanut, and – corn. Fresh fruit sorbets range from *zapote mamey* to quince.

Back in the capital, Morelia, any sweet tooth goes into overdrive at the Mercado de Dulces, a specialist market tucked away behind a Jesuit convent. Each stand is piled high with Morelia's famous *ates* (fruit pastes of guava, pineapple, or quince), sugared figs, tamarinds in chili powder, fudge, fruit-flavored *piloncillo* (unrefined sugar), coconut in syrup, and finally *morelianas* (thin wafers of caramelized sugar, milk, and vanilla). It is a calorific cornucopia, though no more so than the city's nucleus of upmarket restaurants, nearly all cannily combining the past with the present: Purépecha along with Spanish and Mexican ingredients and techniques. Encouraged by a constant influx of foreigners coming through its international airport and a lively cultural calendar, Morelia is far from lagging behind in the *nueva cocina* stakes. Above all, though, it wallows comfortably in a fair and fertile land.

victor hugo martinez
la conspiración

With a name like Victor Hugo you might expect this chef's dishes to have a Gallic bent. Not so. Victor's main inspiration comes straight from coastal Michoacán and has woven into his dishes at La Conspiración, a restaurant and oyster bar that opened four years ago. "We started with a basic menu which we gradually refined," he explains. "Sometimes I just change how a classic dish looks – it's surprising how much that affects people's perception." And he is adamant about the direction of Mexican cuisine. "It is definitely changing – but not the ingredients. It is all about presentation."

So did his parents realize what associations they were baptizing him with? "No!" laughs the ever upbeat Victor. "Not at all. Very few people know the name of the French writer here." Given the colonial time capsule that is Morelia, this is hardly surprising. The restaurant is different, though, as it blends a 17th-century structure with informal Mexican modernity. Background jazz competes with the toll of the cathedral bells outside; boyish waiters in lime-green shirts whisk plates around and the walls are hung with contemporary paintings. It's obviously a winning formula as, during the long lunch session, the three interconnecting dining rooms are buzzing. Regulars include the state governor along with his bodyguards.

Victor claims to have tasted his first chili at the age of four. "This is quite typical for a Mexican – I love chilies," he chuckles.

"We put them in absolutely everything to add sharpness." So how did he learn his trade? "My mother was an excellent cook. I was one of 10 children and as she had to prepare three meals a day for us she virtually lived in the kitchen. I always helped out, so learned a lot. Then when I was 20 I did a three-year cooking course in Manzanillo, on the coast."

In the kitchen, a team of eight permanent staff is occasionally joined by student apprentices. "I teach teenagers at a technical school a couple of mornings a week," he continues. "Other mornings I'll go to the market. I buy everything there, see new products and let the ideas flow. When I experiment, first I taste the dish myself then I test it on friends whose palates I trust. They've got to be honest though!"

A strong emphasis on seafood means that his menu offers no fewer than nine different shrimp dishes and a further nine with red snapper. Is there ever any seafood fatigue? Victor's eyes roll expressively. "Not at all! I've always loved seafood and go to the coast whenever I can, to places like Ixtapa and Puerto Vallarta where you can eat really well. One day, when I can afford it, I know I'll go to Venice and Paris." At last the romantic speaks, living up to his name.

tarascan chili bean soup
sopa tarasca

Victor's wholesome Tarascan soup combines classic flavors with a scattering of additions like the *tortilla* strips (similar to *Sopa Azteca*), cheese, and avocado. Vary the quantities to make the soup more or less filling.

Fry the *tortilla* strips in a little oil until crisp. Remove, lay on paper towels to absorb any excess oil, and set aside.

Lightly fry the *ancho* chili strips in a little oil.

In a food processor, blend the tomatoes, onion, garlic, and fried *ancho* chili strips, reserving a handful of strips for garnishing, to a smooth purée. Set aside.

Blend the bean purée, half the *tortilla* strips, and the chicken stock in a food processor. Pour this and the tomato mixture into a saucepan, stir well, season with salt, and simmer with a lid on for about 10 minutes.

Serve hot in individual soup bowls, topped with a spoonful of crème fraîche and accompanied by a plate of cheese cubes, the remaining *tortilla* and *ancho* chili strips, and the avocado slices.

serves 4–6

6 corn *tortillas*, cut into short strips

peanut or corn oil

3 *ancho* chilies, cut into strips

7oz (200g) tomatoes, seeded and roughly chopped

1 small onion, peeled and roughly chopped

2 garlic cloves, peeled

9oz (250g) beans (any type except black), cooked and puréed

3½ pints (2 liters) chicken stock

salt, to taste

9fl oz (250ml) crème fraîche

9oz (250g) firm, fresh cheese like mozzarella, cut into small cubes

1 large avocado, peeled, pitted, and sliced lengthwise

sweetcorn *tamales*
uchepos

Soft, sweet, and creamy, this street-food classic makes a great
form of stuffing (see opposite).

Blend the sweetcorn to a paste in a food processor.

In a large bowl, cream the butter and stir in a tablespoonful of the *masa harina* and the chicken
stock alternately. Stir in the sugar, salt, and baking powder, then gradually mix in the sweetcorn
paste.

Place two tablespoons of the mixture in each corn husk and fold over the sides, then the ends,
to form a neat parcel. Arrange in a steamer and cook for 1–1½ hours. Open when the dough
separates easily from the wrapping.

To make the cream sauce, mix together the cream, chicken bouillon powder, and chopped
parsley in a small saucepan and heat gently without boiling.

Serve the *uchepos* immediately with the cream sauce.

serves 4

8oz (225g) cooked fresh
   sweetcorn kernels

1½oz (40g) butter

1½oz (40g) *masa harina* (Mexican
   corn flour)

2–3 tbsp chicken stock

1 tsp superfine sugar

pinch of salt

pinch of baking powder

8 corn husks from around the cobs,
   soaked in water for 15 minutes
   (or use parchment paper)

for the cream sauce

18fl oz (500ml) heavy cream

1 tsp chicken bouillon powder

1 tsp chopped fresh flat-leaf parsley

Mixing sweet and sour, this surprising recipe combines the rich flavor of dark red *ancho* chilies with a sweet, soft corn stuffing, made from *uchepos* (see opposite), and a cream sauce: not for dieters but it makes a sumptuous vegetarian dish.

michoacán stuffed *ancho* chilies
chiles michoacanos

To make the *uchepos*, follow the recipe opposite. Allow them to cool then chop into small pieces and set aside.

Rinse the chilies, then slit them carefully down one side, remove the seeds and veins, and pat the outside dry. Heat the oil in a frying pan and fry the chilies for a few minutes, turning frequently.

Pour 1¾ pints (1 liter) of water into a large saucepan, add the sugar, and bring to a boil. Drop in the fried chilies, turn off the heat, and leave the peppers to soak for about 5 minutes or until they soften. Drain and set aside.

Melt the butter in a frying pan and fry the pieces of *uchepos*. Stir in the cheese, half & half, and chicken bouillon powder and heat through gently without boiling. Sprinkle over the parsley and remove from the heat.

To make the cream sauce, follow the recipe opposite.

Fill the chilies with the cheese and *uchepo* mixture and serve immediately, smothered in hot creamy sauce.

serves 5

5 large *ancho* **chilies**

8fl oz (225 ml) **vegetable oil**

3 tbsp **superfine sugar**

3 tbsp **butter**

14oz (400g) *uchepos* **(see opposite)**

5¼oz (150g) **feta cheese**

5fl oz (150ml) **half & half**

1 tsp **chicken bouillon powder**

1 tsp **chopped fresh parsley**

18fl oz (500ml) **cream sauce (see opposite)**

This beautiful dish has a delicate air about it that is completely belied by the heat of the chili. Although *jalapeño* is one of the milder types, you may want to reduce the quantity. This makes a perfect appetizer for a hot summer's day – washed down with a cool Mexican beer.

marinated shrimp
ceviche de camarones en aguachile

Place the shrimp in a non-metallic bowl and pour over the lemon juice. Add the remaining ingredients, season with salt and pepper, and leave to marinate for 15 minutes.

Serve with savory Mexican-style crackers or toast.

serves 4

1lb 5oz (600g) large raw shrimp, cleaned and butterflied

1¼ pints (700ml) fresh lemon juice

13oz (375g) cucumber, peeled, seeded, and thinly sliced into semicircles

12 *jalapeño* chilies, seeded, deveined, and cut into strips

1 red onion, peeled and chopped into thin strips

salt and freshly ground black pepper

michoacán steak tartare
carne apache

As one of Mexico's most rural states, Michoacán abounds with cowboys. They would love this dish as it is fresh, energizing, and easy to prepare and to eat. Serve with toast or Mexican-style crackers, then hit the road.

Stir together the beef and the lemon juice in a non-metallic dish and leave to marinate for 15–20 minutes.

Stir in the tomatoes, onion, cilantro, and chilies. Season with salt and pepper.

Arrange on a plate and top with the avocado slices.

serves 4

1lb 2oz (500g) good-quality organic lean ground beef

7fl oz (200ml) fresh lemon juice

5¼oz (150g) tomatoes, finely chopped

2 large onions, peeled and finely chopped

large bunch fresh cilantro, finely chopped

2oz (55g) *serrano* chilies, seeded, deveined, and finely chopped

salt and freshly ground black pepper

1 ripe Hass avocado, peeled, pitted, and sliced

milk and cinnamon cream dessert
chongos zamoranos

Ideally, *chongos* should be cooked in a *cazuela*, a traditional earthenware casserole that imparts a special flavor. This dessert is a much loved childhood pudding and exists in numerous canned versions, but this is the real thing.

Pour the milk into a shallow, flameproof dish. Add the sugar and stir over low heat until it has completely dissolved. Add the rennet, cover with a lid or some foil, and set aside at room temperature for 2 hours until the mixture has set.

With a sharp knife, cut into 1 or 2-inch (2.5–5cm) squares in the dish and stick a sliver of cinnamon stick in each one.

Cook over very low heat for 8 hours so that the milk caramelizes and turns golden. Cool before serving.

serves 4–6

3½ pints (2 liters) whole milk

1lb 5oz (600g) superfine sugar

6 drops of liquid rennet

3½oz (100g) cinnamon sticks, slivered

morelian cheesecake with guava
pay moreliano

María biscuits crop up quite often in Mexican recipes as they are the standard commercial brand. Use any plain sweet biscuit – rich tea or digestive – in their place. Guavas are popular in Michoacán and the subtly flavored, jelly-like paste finds its way into numerous desserts.

Preheat the oven to 325ºF/170ºC.

To make the base, crush the biscuits to fine crumbs either in a food processor or by hand, in a plastic bag with a rolling pin. Mix in the butter and the egg. Press the mixture into the bottom of a buttered 9-inch round or springform cake pan.

Cover the crumb base with the pieces of guava paste.

Beat the remaining ingredients together until well blended. Pour over the biscuit and guava base. Bake for 25 minutes until lightly set.

Remove from oven and leave to cool before serving.

serves 8–10

for the base

2 packets María biscuits, about 9oz (250g)

3oz (85g) butter, softened

1 large egg

for the topping

1lb 9oz (700g) roll of guava paste, chopped

7oz (200ml) can condensed milk

3½oz (100g) cream cheese

4 large eggs

ruben cruz
la azotea

"I've worked here for nine years without a holiday," Ruben Cruz announces, looking around La Azotea, a style-conscious modern restaurant crowning a period mansion in the heart of Morelia. The rooftop restaurant is a world away from the floors below, with their stone arches, huge doors and windows, and baroque details. Designed as a Bishop's Palace in 1700, the building became a monastery before the latest of several makeovers transformed it in 1998.

However, for this workaholic chef, all these features are irrelevant. His focus is 100 percent on the food and its preparation. "I started cooking when I was 16 in my hometown of Querétaro," he explains. "My mother was a great cook and famous for her *mole*, but I was first drawn to making cakes. Then I worked in Manzanillo and also at the Camino Real in Mexico City for a year. It's a laborious career with long hours. You've really got to like it." Yet somehow, this ultra-focused man in his mid-50s has had time to have eight children, including Adrian, 25, who has worked beside him for over seven years and takes over when Ruben is away on a gastronomic trip.

Looking at his menu, it is clear that Ruben's influences go way beyond Michoacán. "I like preparing what's difficult, not what's easy," he continues. "I have a lot of old classics on the menu like Veracruz-style red snapper or paté and I've just developed a pre-Hispanic dish of snails fried with butter, onion, green chili, cilantro, and salt. It comes from Hidalgo, but unfortunately it's only feasible in March when snails are best and plentiful."

Other dishes using typical Mexican ingredients are his beef filet with *nopal* (cactus leaf), a sauce combining five chilies, and a divine dessert of sliced *jícama* (a juicy root vegetable similar to turnip) in a caramel syrup and flambéd in tequila. "Morelians come here for special occasions but we get a lot of tourists – Americans, Japanese, and Europeans – on a regular basis too." he says proudly. "Some Spaniards were so happy with my food that they offered me a job in Andalucia!"

In the kitchen, 13 people work steadily while blenders and grinders whirr, knives chop in a staccato rhythm, and corn in its husk slowly blackens over the coals. Ruben dexterously slices the grain off a corn cob. "I go to the local market myself but order special ingredients like cherries and duck from Querétaro, and seafood comes straight up from the coast. We try to work mostly with local produce as it's always the best." Then he turns back to the job in hand: nothing else matters.

filo pastry with ricotta and zucchini flowers
phyllo relleno de queso de cabra y flor de calabaza

This appetizer is warm and crisp with subtle flavors of zucchini flowers and avocado. Goat's cheese gives the dish more bite, but ricotta has the perfect texture to be used as a substitute.

To make the zucchini flower stuffing, melt the butter in a frying pan and sauté the onion and garlic until the onion is softened but not browned. Then stir in the zucchini flowers with a pinch of salt, mix well, and heat until the flowers start to wilt.

Preheat the oven to 425°F/220°C.

Brush the pastry with half the melted butter. Cover with a layer of the stuffing and then spread a layer of cheese on top. Roll up carefully and place, seam-side down, on a baking sheet. Brush with the remaining melted butter and bake for 15–20 minutes.

While the pastries are cooking, blend all the ingredients for the avocado sauce in a blender or food processor to form a smooth purée.

Remove the pastries from the oven. Slice each one diagonally and serve hot with a generous drizzle of avocado sauce.

serves 6

6 rectangular sheets of filo pastry, roughly 6¼ in x 4in (16cm x 10cm)

2–3 tbsp butter, melted

5½oz (150g) fresh goat's cheese or ricotta, mashed

for the zucchini flower stuffing

2 tbsp butter

1 tbsp peeled and chopped onion

1 garlic clove, peeled and crushed

salt, to taste

5¼oz (150g) zucchini flowers, rinsed and roughly chopped

for the avocado sauce

1 avocado, about 7oz (200g), peeled, pitted, and mashed

1 medium onion, peeled and roughly chopped

4–5 sprigs of fresh cilantro, leaves only

1 tbsp chopped *tomatillos*

1–2 tsp chopped green chilies

3½fl oz (100ml) chicken stock

salt, to taste

mestizo soup
sopa mestiza

In Mexican, the word *mestizo* crops up again and again, referring to people of mixed Spanish and indigenous blood. Here is it applied to a nourishing soup of mixed vegetables, made truly Mexican by a fiery edge of *chipotle* chilies.

Heat the oil in a large saucepan and sauté the leeks, celery, carrots, onions, mushrooms, sweetcorn, zucchini flowers, and garlic until tender.

Add the tomatoes, chilies, *epazote,* and chicken stock and bring to a boil. Add salt to taste, and serve piping hot.

serves 6

2 tbsp vegetable oil

2½oz (70g) each of chopped leeks, celery, and carrots

1 small onion, peeled and roughly chopped

1oz (25g) mushrooms, sliced

1½oz (40g) cooked sweetcorn kernels, fresh or canned

1½oz (40g) zucchini flowers, rinsed

2 garlic cloves, peeled and crushed

2lb 4oz (1kg) tomatoes, skinned and finely chopped

1 tsp chopped canned *chipotle* chilies

1 tsp fresh chopped *epazote* or flat-leaf parsley

3 pints (1.7 liters) chicken stock

salt, to taste

Morelia is famous for its crystallized and preserved fruits found in incredible variety at the Mercado de Dulces (sweet market). Quince works perfectly with this recipe as its flavor marries so well with cheese.

baked quince and cheese rolls
rollo de ate y queso

Preheat the oven to 400°F/200°C.

Brush the pastry sheets with half of the melted butter and spread a layer of quince paste over each, then cover with a layer of cheese. Roll up the pastry and place, seam-side down, on a baking sheet. Brush with the remaining melted butter and bake for 15–20 minutes.

To serve, make a few diagonal slashes in each roll and dust with a sifting of confectioners' sugar.

serves 2–3

6 rectangular sheets of filo pastry roughly 6¼in x 4in (16cm x 10cm)

1oz (25g) butter, melted

5½oz (150g) quince paste

5¼oz (150g) fresh cheese such as feta, ricotta, or soft goat's cheese

1 tbsp confectioners' sugar

Ruben brought this recipe with him from his hometown of Querétaro, a region where berries are abundant. Steamed in this way, the duck becomes ultra-tender. Serve it with wild rice and crunchy piles of finely sliced and sautéed leeks.

duck in black cherry sauce
pato en salsa de cereza negra

Preheat oven to 400°F/200°C.

Wash the duck, pat dry with paper towels, then brush lightly with oil and sprinkle with salt, pepper, and rosemary.

Arrange all the vegetables at the bottom of a roasting pan and lay the duck on top. Pour 1 pint (600ml) of water into the roasting pan, cover with aluminum foil, and place in the oven for about 3 hours.

Meanwhile, make the black cherry sauce. Heat the cranberry purée in a saucepan and flambé with the brandy. Add the wine, bring to a boil, then stir in the honey and black cherries. Cook over low heat for around 5 minutes until the cherries are hot and slightly softened. Stir in the brown sauce and butter and mix well.

To serve, carve the duck into four portions and serve on individual plates with the black cherry sauce poured on top.

serves 4

1 duck, about 2lb 1oz (1.25 kg)

3½fl oz (100ml) vegetable oil

salt and freshly ground black pepper

2–3 tsp chopped fresh rosemary

3½oz (100g) carrots, peeled and
  cut into chunks

3½oz (100g) leeks, thickly sliced

3½oz (100g) celery, thickly sliced

2 medium onions, peeled and
  roughly chopped

for the black cherry sauce

1lb 2oz (500g) cranberry purée

2 tbsp brandy

9fl oz (250ml) red wine

3½fl oz (100ml) runny honey

10½oz (300g) pitted fresh
  black cherries

5fl oz (150ml) brown sauce

3½oz (100g) butter

In Ruben's version, you can taste the smokiness of his barbecued sweetcorn, but even if you use the canned variety the delicious *huitlacoche* (corn truffle) still adds plenty of flavor. This substantial dish can be served with mashed potato and sautéed leeks.

beef with *huitlacoche* sauce
medallones rellenos de granos de elote en salsa de huitlacoche

Cut the filet into 6 equal rounds, weighing about 6oz (175g) each. Slit each one to make a pocket and fill this with 1oz (25g) of the corn kernels.

To make the *huitlacoche* sauce, sauté the onion, garlic, chili, and tomatoes in olive oil until softened.

Add the *huitlacoches* and cook until the mixture is just starting to bubble. Remove from the heat and season with salt and pepper.

Broil the beef rounds on both sides until cooked to your preference. Arrange on individual plates and spoon over the *huitlacoche* sauce.

serves 6

2lb 4oz (1kg) filet of beef

5¼oz (150g) cooked sweetcorn
  kernels, fresh or canned

for the huitlacoche (corn
truffle) sauce

1 small onion, peeled and
  finely chopped

1 garlic clove, peeled and crushed

1 green chili, seeded, deveined,
  and finely chopped

2 medium tomatoes, finely chopped

2fl oz (50ml) olive oil

15oz (425g) *huitlacoches*
  (corn truffles), mashed

salt and freshly ground black pepper

Piloncillo (unrefined sugar), sold in cones, is loved by Mexican cooks as it gives a natural sweetness that has far more flavor than refined white sugar. Muscovado sugar, with its high molasses content, comes very close.

doughnuts with brown sugar syrup
buñuelos con miel de piloncillo

Pile up the flour on a large chopping board or clean work surface, or use a bowl if you prefer. Make a hollow in the middle and pour in the sugar, yeast, salt, oil, and 2fl oz (50ml) of tepid water. Work the mixture with your hands, kneading well, until all the ingredients are thoroughly mixed and form a smooth ball of dough. Then work in the butter.

Divide the dough into 12 equal pieces. Roll each into a ball between your palms and flatten slightly into a round with a rolling pin. Line a baking sheet with parchment paper and arrange the dough balls on top, leaving plenty of room between each one. Cover loosely with a sheet of oiled plastic wrap and set aside in a warm place for 45–60 minutes until well-risen and almost doubled in size.

Meanwhile, make the syrup by dissolving the sugar in 9fl oz (250ml) of water over low heat, simmering until the liquid thickens to a honey-like consistency.

Heat the oil in a large deep saucepan to a temperature of 325°F/160°C. Press your thumb into the center of each dough ball to make a small indentation. Carefully fry a few dough balls at a time until golden. Lift out of the oil with a slotted spoon and lay on paper towels to absorb any excess oil.

Mix the sugar and cinnamon and toss the doughnuts in it until well coated.

Serve drizzled with syrup and scattered with fresh berries.

serves 6

4oz (115g) all-purpose flour

2 tsp superfine sugar

1 tsp instant or rapid-rise yeast

pinch of salt

1 tbsp vegetable oil

2½ tbsp softened butter

9fl oz (250ml) vegetable oil

5 tbsp superfine sugar

3 tbsp ground cinnamon

9oz (250g) fresh seasonal berries such as strawberries, raspberries, or blueberries

for the sugar loaf syrup

4½oz (125g) sugar loaf (*piloncillo*) or muscovado sugar

market food

morelia's street snacks

With 40,000 students tearing through the delightful 16th–18th-century streets and shady plazas of Morelia's city center, street food is as easy to find as cyber-cafés, bars, and churches. One central snacking area lies in the shadow of San Agustín, one of Morelia's earliest monuments, on Calle Corregidora and Abasolo. Here, under the arcades in what was once a monastery cloister, hot food is dished up daily at folding tables. The *al fresco* venue attracts students, young couples, and even families, who tuck into generous *quesadillas* and *tortas*.

With dusk comes a new arrival, Enrique, whose modest stall is framed by an archway with a view of San Agustín. Enrique is the popular local purveyor of *uchepo*s, quintessential Michoacán fare made from tender young corn kernels that are mashed, sweetened, then steamed in fresh corn husks like *tamale*s (see page 108). Enrique makes two versions: an ultra-simple one that merely adds sugar to the corn mash, and another, much richer one combining cream, sugar, and cinnamon. Children in particular love unpeeling the corn wrapping to discover the soft, creamy filling inside.

Morelia's other big hit in the realm of street food is the *gaspacho*. Bizarrely, it has nothing in common with Andalucia's famous chilled vegetable soup: here it assumes the form of a highly nutritious fruit salad, spiced up with chili sauce, enriched with cheese, sharpened with lime juice, and finally doused in orange juice. Altogether, it is an unusual combination of cooling fruit with a chili hit and, unlike *uchepos,* will not pile on the pounds. On Avenida Morelos, the traffic-choked east–west axis, and just a few doors from the illustrious college of San Nicolas, every morning José Roberto Reyes chops huge quantities of fruit in readiness for the student lunchtime rush.

morelian gaspacho

Jícama, a slightly bland but very crisp, juicy tuber native to Mexico, is readily available in California but not in the rest of the United States. It is a classic street snack all over Mexico, usually eaten sliced, sprinkled with salt, lime, and chili powder. In this refreshing *gaspacho,* the *jícama* could be replaced by two or three small, very young turnips. It should be prepared at the last minute so that it does not become soggy.

In a bowl, mix the mangoes, pineapple, and *jícama* together with the chili powder, chili sauce, and salt.

Pour over the lime juice, sprinkle with cheese, and douse in orange juice. Serve in tall glasses.

serves 6

3 ripe but firm mangoes, peeled, pitted, and diced

1 large pineapple, peeled, cored, and diced

1 *jícama,* peeled and diced

1–2 tsp chili powder, according to taste

2–3 tbsp chili sauce, according to taste

pinch of salt

juice of 1 lime

3oz (85g) sharp white cheese, such as Wensleydale or Cheddar, grated

juice of 3 oranges

Scrubby mesquite bushes and thousands of cacti spike the rugged hillsides of the Valley of Oaxaca, hardly propitious for one of Mexico's greatest gastronomic destinations. Yet this is the scenery that surrounds the city of seven *moles* and is also the source of *mezcal*, that rival of tequila with a worm lodged in its bottle. Oaxaca is known for its intense Indian soul and character, forged by 16 different indigenous groups each with millennia-old histories, 150 dialects, very little *mestizaje*, and 30 of Mexico's 50 types of corn. The combination of this indigenous character and the luminous state capital has always attracted a shifting community of writers and artists. Inspired by fantastic ingredients, *nueva cocina* flourishes. Grasshoppers, zucchini flowers, and cactus leaves are just the tip of a delicious culinary iceberg.

Oaxaca state's feuding Zapotecs and Mixtecs, the two largest indigenous groups, not only built stunning structures like Monte Alban and Mitla but also cultivated the great pre-Hispanic trinity of squash, corn, and beans in the Oaxaca valley. From the lush north of the state comes tropical fruit while south, beyond the folds of the Sierra Madre del Sur, lies the balmy Pacific coast. In sybaritic resorts like Puerto Escondido and Huatulco, red snapper, squid, and blue crabs are hauled in daily. Farther east, the offbeat culture of the Isthmus favors iguana *tamales* washed down with *horchata de coco* (coconut rice milk) or just a crisp, cool beer; party fever here is notoriously contagious. But it is in the center of the state that the most refined and complex cuisine has developed.

Rotating weekly markets in the main Valley towns (where in some cases the barter system still survives) and six daily ones in Oaxaca city itself dominate daily life and are mainly orchestrated by the Zapotecs. A hedonistic community named after a local plum, the *zapote*, they are forceful characters. Even behind market stalls, the sturdy women wear dazzling embroidered *huipiles*, satin ribbons braided into their hair (a style made famous by the artist Frida Kahlo), and still manage to balance their wares on top of their heads. Oaxaca's Central de Abastos, said to be the largest indigenous market in Latin America, is the Zapotecs' shadowy, mysterious heartland. The background murmur of their voices, once lyrically described by D H Lawrence as "like rain, or banana leaves in the wind," is punctuated by squawks of turkeys, guinea pigs, and rabbits, all destined for *la cazuela* (casserole), as well as determined sales pitches from the women vendors.

In the pungent *comedores* (eateries) you can grab a bag of high-protein fried *chapulines* (grasshoppers) sprinkled with lime and chili powder, savor a *tamal* steamed in banana leaves, or feast on highly flavored goat stew. Beyond are twisting alleyways showcasing *quesillos* (balls of stringy cheese similar to mozzarella), neat pyramids of colored *mole* pastes, *tlayudas* (giant, platter-like *tortillas* sold out of sacks), *tasajo* (curtains of freshly hammered and stretched beef), pigs' heads, vertiginous mounds of pomegranates, watermelons, a gigantic local tamarind – and, of course, no Mexican market is worth its salt without chilies.

The local favorite is the *pasilla*, whose hot, smoky flavor and deep red color is combined with chocolate, toasted *chilhuacles*, and *mulato* chilies in *mole negro*, the number one of Oaxaca's famed seven *moles*. And the other six? They are *amarillo* (mild and yellow from cumin), *coloradito* (brick-red from *ancho* chilies and tomatoes), *almendrado* (with almonds), *verde* (green from pumpkin seeds and *hoja santa*), *de Castillo* (*guajillo* chilies, bread, and black pepper), *manchamanteles* (sweet and fruity), and *chichilo* (rich, dark, and ultra-smoky). But many Oaxacans own up to buying their *moles* in paste or powder form because they are so complicated and time-consuming to make at home.

The foodie path continues through Oaxaca's arcaded 17th-century *zócalo* (central city square) with its lofty trees, bandstand, magnificent cathedral, women selling fragrant gardenias and roses, and streetwise kids dodging the tourist police. Beyond are facades of carved green stone or houses painted in rainbow hues, the extraordinary baroque interior of Santo Domingo church and a string of hip restaurants and boutiques. Sensuality is everywhere, in smell, sound, taste, and sight, so it is no surprise that Oaxaca has nurtured artists, from painters Rufino Tamayo and Francisco Toledo to contemporary singers like Lila Downs. Foreign writers, too, have been seduced: D H Lawrence in the 1920s, Aldous Huxley in the 1930s, and in the 1980s, Italo Calvino, who penned his "gustatory exploration" in *Under the Jaguar Sun* (1992).

Calvino's fertile imagination could well have been touched by ice cream flavors such as rose petal, soursop (a fruit with a fragrant but sharp creamy flesh), *leche quemada* (literally "burnt milk"), *mezcal* and prickly pear, washed down by cool, colorful *aguas frescas*, from *horchata* (rice water, cinnamon, almonds, and prickly pear purée) to *chilacayote* (winter squash), mango, and of course, plum. Oaxaca's quintessential drink, however, is chocolate, that old Olmec, Aztec, and Maya favorite. Specialist companies sell blocks of cooking chocolate at the central market, Mercado 20 de Noviembre, although real aficionados search out homemade versions, *xocolate de metate*, sold by little women from their baskets.

With such a heritage of good food, Oaxaca is producing some fantastic chefs – led by Alejandro Ruíz, a true man of the Valley – who find their inspiration in the plethora of traditional ingredients and flavors available in the locality. With a steady flow of foreigners hungry for new yet authentic tastes, innovative cooking confirms Oaxaca's status as Mexico's most sophisticated city for indiginous fare.

alejandro ruíz olmedo
casa oaxaca

Alejandro Ruíz oozes such energy, charm, and bonhomie that the moment he arrives at the mellow, arty setting of Casa Oaxaca the whole restaurant seems to light up. Proud to be a man of Oaxaca, born and bred in the Valley, Alejandro has overcome humble beginnings to attain international status, yet he still comments modestly, "I've been finding my way all this time."

The whitewashed walls of his restaurant and, a few blocks away, the associated boutique hotel where he started a decade ago, are where he hones his sophisticated cuisine. "Cooking is an adventure – sometimes it works, sometimes it doesn't, but you have to experiment. I'm self-taught, so I have no rules." He smiles. It is this intuitive, wild-child side to Alejandro that, coupled with great determination, has shattered Oaxacan norms. Yet although playing audaciously with Mediterranean and Mexican ingredients, he preserves the scents and flavors of his locale. Olive oil, garlic, and onion sit side by side with lime, avocado, and the semi-mythical *hoja santa* herb. And true to Oaxaca's marked artistic bent, every plate is a picture – accompanied by huge blue-corn *totopos* (crisp, sculptural *tortillas*).

The land has always fed his soul. "I was born into a small community of about 100 families who were all farmers with goats or who grew vegetables. I even worked as a goat- and cow-herd as a boy. That rural upbringing meant good, fresh food was part of me right from the start. My mother taught us to eat well but it was my grandmother who was the really fantastic cook. I was the eldest of five so helped out a lot after my mother died when I was 12. One of my younger brothers followed me and is the manager here.

"At 15 I started off as a dishwasher before becoming a waiter. Eventually, I started cooking. At one point I spent a year in Berlin at the famous Vatu restaurant. Bizarrely, that was where I learned to cook fish – from a chef who'd worked in Italy! Otherwise my teachers have always been the market women selling spices and herbs here in Oaxaca. Their knowledge is extraordinary. I go to the Valley markets as often as I can."

Ask him which place has most inspired him on his travels and the answer is instantaneous: "San Sebastian! It is a paradise for chefs and good food. In fact Juan Mari Arzak has become a friend of mine." He is referring to Spain's king of *nuevo coquina*. "But things are changing in Mexico too. Only 15 years ago, it was women chefs who led the restaurant revolution. Now it's men!" he adds triumphantly.

Does he ever slow down? "Two things help me relax," he concedes. "Cinema and football. I'm the goalie in a team of carpenters and bus drivers out in my village. When we play on Sundays, that brings me down to earth." So the balance that Alejandro has created in his cooking seems to be an integral facet of his life.

fava bean soup
sopa de habas

serves 4

2 tbsp vegetable oil

1 small onion, peeled and finely chopped

1 garlic clove, peeled and crushed

2 tomatoes, chopped

14oz (400g) dried fava beans (yellow in color), cooked in salted water

7oz (200g) cooked chickpeas, skinned, or canned

7oz (200g) corn kernels, cooked in salted water, or canned

16 medium dried shrimp

1¾ pints (1 liter) fish consommé or water

salt and freshly ground black pepper

2 tbsp chopped fresh cilantro, to garnish

In a large saucepan, heat the oil and sauté the onion and garlic for about 1 minute. Add the tomatoes and cook for a couple of minutes over low heat.

Mash the tomatoes with a fork then add the beans, chickpeas, corn, shrimp, and fish consommé. Bring to a boil, reduce the heat, and simmer for about 10 minutes. Season with salt and pepper to taste and garnish with a sprinkling of cilantro.

With flavors that far surpass its humble name, this soup is a typically multi-layered Alejandro concoction. Like chickpeas, fava beans are not native to Mexico but started life in the Arab world.

tuna with soy sauce
atún en salsa de soja

This divine fusion dish mixes the Asian-derived flavor of soy sauce with North African citrus juice and typically Mexican zucchini flowers. It should be served immediately, with steamed white rice and fresh tomatoes.

In a large frying pan, heat the olive oil for 1 minute, then quickly sear the tuna filets on high heat for 1 minute on each side. Add the garlic and fry for 30 seconds until just golden. Pour in the soy sauce and the fruit juices, then remove the tuna from the frying pan and set aside.

Lower the heat and continue to cook the sauce for another minute until all the ingredients are well blended and the sauce is slightly reduced, then stir in the butter.

Place the tuna filets on individual plates, then dip the zucchini flowers in the soy sauce mixture and place one on top of each filet. Bathe the tuna with the remaining sauce.

serves 4

2fl oz (50ml) olive oil

1lb 12oz (800g) fresh tuna, cut into 4 equal filets

12 garlic cloves, peeled and crushed

9fl oz (250ml) soy sauce

4fl oz (125ml) fresh lemon juice

3½fl oz (100ml) fresh orange juice

3½oz (100g) butter

4 zucchini flowers, rinsed

ceviche-stuffed chilies with passion fruit sauce
chiles rellenos de ceviche con salsa de maracuyá

Extreme and intense flavors make Alejandro's take on a stuffed chili out of this world. The sauce is very sweet and can be diluted with water if you prefer.

Mix the lemon juice and oregano in a non-metallic dish. Add the sea bream and marinate in the refrigerator for about 5 hours.

Toast the chilies over a flame, on a griddle, or under a broiler until the skins are charred. Put in a plastic bag to sweat for 15 minutes then peel off the burnt skin under cold running water. Cut off the stalk, slit the chilies carefully down one side, and remove the seeds and veins. Set aside.

Place the muscovado sugar, mango, passion fruit pulp, and cinnamon stick in a saucepan and simmer over low heat for about 30 minutes, or until the sauce thickens.

Stir the cilantro and tomatoes into the marinated fish then fill the chilies with this mixture. To serve, spoon some passion fruit sauce onto each plate, and place a stuffed chili on top. Scatter over pomegranate seeds to garnish.

serves 8

2 tbsp fresh lemon juice

1 tsp dried oregano

1lb 4oz (550g) fresh sea bream filets, cut into small cubes

8 *poblano* chilies or bell peppers

1¾oz (50g) muscovado sugar

1 large ripe mango, peeled, pitted, and diced

7oz (200g) passion fruit pulp

½ cinnamon stick

small bunch of fresh cilantro, finely chopped

2–3 ripe tomatoes, finely chopped

seeds from half a pomegranate, to garnish

fish filet with lemon, capers, and zucchini flowers
filete de pescado al limón con alcaparras y flor de calabaza

The crisp skin and soft flesh of the fish contrasts beautifully with the sauce with its sharp bite of capers and lemon. The big surprise here is the sweet tomato marmalade.

First prepare the marmalade. Preheat the oven to 400°F/200°C. Place the tomatoes in a roasting pan, pour over the honey and olive oil, add the rosemary and season with salt and pepper. Roast for 45 minutes.

Remove the tomatoes from the oven. If any juice remains, boil over high heat until any liquid has evaporated. Set aside.

Season the fish filets with salt and pepper and rub over the garlic. Heat the olive oil in a frying pan. When hot, fry the filets for about 2 minutes on each side or until the skin is golden and the flesh has cooked all the way through. Add the capers, lemon juice, and butter and heat through. Add the zucchini flowers at the last minute so they are just wilted.

To serve, spoon some marmalade onto the center of each plate and place a fish filet on top. Pour the caper sauce over the filet and arrange the zucchini flowers around it.

serves 4

for the fish filets

4 red snapper or grouper filets, about 7oz (200g) each

salt and freshly ground black pepper

1 small garlic clove, peeled and crushed

5 tbsp olive oil

2oz (55g) capers

2fl oz (55ml) fresh lemon juice

3oz (85g) butter

12 zucchini flowers, rinsed

for the tomato marmalade

1lb 12oz (800g) tomatoes, skinned, quartered, and seeded

2 tbsp runny honey

2 tbsp olive oil

1 sprig of fresh rosemary

salt and freshly ground pepper

Succulent and flavorsome venison, a classic pre-Hispanic meat, has made a big comeback among new-wave Mexican chefs as it is a lot less fatty than beef. Deer are native to Mexico although, as they are now protected, imported venison has to be used. Alejandro serves this dish with a pumpkin purée and fresh asparagus (when in season), cooked *al dente*, although a simple salad and some potatoes would be equally good.

venison in *achiote*, orange, and rosemary sauce
venado al achiote y jugo de naranja con romero

Preheat the oven to 450°F/230°C.

In a mixing bowl, whisk the *achiote* paste into the orange juice. Stir in the onion, garlic, rosemary, bay leaves, a twist of pepper, and the salt.

In a large frying pan, heat the oil and sear the venison on all sides. Then transfer to a casserole and pour over the orange juice mixture. Roast for 10–15 minutes for rare, or 10–15 minutes longer if you prefer your meat well done. Remove the venison from the casserole and set aside.

Return the casserole to the oven, lower the heat to 350ºF/180ºC and continue to cook the juices for another 30 minutes. Then strain the juice into a saucepan and boil over medium heat until it is reduced by half. Adjust the seasoning if necessary and whisk in the butter.

Carve the venison into thin slices and quickly warm them up on a hot griddle or in a frying pan. Serve the meat bathed in the orange and rosemary sauce.

serves 4

3½oz (100g) *achiote* paste

1¾ pints (1 liter) fresh orange juice

1 medium onion, peeled and sliced

1 garlic clove, peeled and crushed

1 sprig of fresh rosemary

6 bay leaves

freshly ground black pepper

1 tsp sea salt

3 tbsp olive oil

2lb 4oz (1kg) filet of venison,
  in one piece

7oz (200g) butter

duck with shallots, thyme, and wild mushrooms
pato en reducción de chalotes, tomillo y hongos silvestres

Only the courageous would dare attempt this rather fiddly recipe, but the result is exquisite and one of Alejandro's *tours de force*. It needs to be prepared the day before.

Preheat the oven to 450°F/230°C.

Rub the ducks with salt and a few of the thyme leaves then roast for about 1 hour 50 minutes or until cooked through. Remove from the oven and leave to cool then carefully pick the meat off the bones, reserving the leg, thigh, and breast meat. Refrigerate the meat and save the bones and wings.

In a large saucepan, heat 2 tablespoons of the oil and fry the duck bones and wings until they are golden, then add the celery, leek, and shallots and fry for 10 minutes. Add 1 pint (600ml) of water, bring to a boil, and cook over medium heat until the liquid is reduced to a quarter of its original volume.

Remove the stock from the heat, strain, cool, and refrigerate overnight.

Remove the grease that has risen to the top of the stock. Pour the stock into a saucepan and slowly bring to a boil. Add the remaining thyme and reduce the stock to a quarter of its original volume to create a rich sauce.

Preheat the oven to 400°F/200°C. Spread out the duck meat in a baking dish, pour over the hot chicken stock, and heat in the oven for 10 minutes.

Meanwhile, heat the remaining oil in a frying pan and fry the potatoes on their cut side until golden. Add the green beans and wild mushrooms and sauté until cooked. Season with salt and pepper to taste and sprinkle with *hoja santa*.

Serve the duck bathed in the sauce and accompanied by the potatoes, green beans, and mushrooms.

serves 4–6

- 2 ducks, about 2lb 1oz (1.25 kg) each, cleaned
- 2 tbsp salt
- 10 sprigs of fresh thyme, leaves stripped off
- 4 tbsp olive oil
- 2 celery stalks, chopped
- 1 leek, chopped
- 1lb 2oz (500g) shallots, peeled and roughly chopped
- 18fl oz (500ml) chicken stock
- 12 small new potatoes, cut in half and parboiled for 10 minutes
- 8oz (225g) string beans, cut in half lengthwise and parboiled for 3 minutes
- 12 wild mushrooms (*tecomate* or porcini)
- salt and freshly ground black pepper
- 1 tbsp shredded *hoja santa*

This is a delicious combination and extremely pretty – a stylish ending to any dinner party. As Oaxaca is ice cream heaven, Alejandro does not make his own. Use any gently perfumed ice cream, maybe sprinkled with rose water and a few organic rose petals. With such crisp, paper-thin pastry, the emphasis is on the unctuous lemon filling.

lemon tart with rose-petal ice cream
tarta de limón con nieve oaxaqueña

Preheat the oven to 400°F/200°C.

To make the pastry dough, mix the flour, sugar, and salt together and form into a mound on a clean work surface or in a bowl, then make a well in the center. Drop the butter into the hollow and rub into the dry ingredients with your fingertips to form fine, yellowish crumbs.

Form a well in the center again and tip in the egg yolk and one tablespoon of cold water. Work the dry ingredients into the liquid, adding a little more water if required, to form a firm dough. Roll out the dough as thinly as possible.

Grease a 9-inch loose-bottom flan pan and line it with the dough, covering the bottom and the sides. Prick the base with a fork, line with parchment paper, and cover with pie weights. Bake for 15 minutes or until the pastry is lightly browned. Remove from the oven, allow to cool, and refrigerate until ready to use.

To prepare the filling, beat the eggs, sugar, crème patissière, and lemon juice until smooth and well blended. Pour into a non-stick saucepan and heat very gently, stirring continuously, to avoid scrambling the eggs. Then simmer and stir for 2 more minutes until thickened. Pour the mixture into a bowl and set aside to cool. When tepid, whisk in the butter. Pour into the pastry shell and refrigerate for at least 2 hours.

Serve with a scoop of rose-petal ice cream, or any other delicately scented ice cream, and a squiggle of raspberry coulis. Garnish with a mint leaf and wafer.

serves 10

for the pastry
9oz (250g) flour
1oz (25g) confectioners' sugar
1 tsp salt
4½oz (125g) butter
1 egg yolk, beaten

for the filling
10 eggs
14oz (400g) superfine sugar
1½oz (40g) crème patissière or
   good-quality ready-made custard
7fl oz (200g) fresh lemon juice
10½oz (300g) butter, softened
rose-petal or other delicately
   scented ice cream
raspberry coulis
mint leaves, to garnish
wafer biscuits, to garnish

miguel jiménez
los danzantes

With a name derived from enigmatic glyphs carved at the nearby site of Monte Alban, Los Danzantes evokes the pre-Hispanic universe. Ever since it opened in Coyoacán (a district of Mexico City) 12 years ago, it hit the right groundbreaking formula: modern Mexican cuisine, locally sourced ingredients, and cool restaurant design. Chef Miguel Jiménez then migrated south and for the last five years has headed up the kitchen team at Oaxaca's branch.

In his early 30s, Miguel is dedicated and serious about his craft yet appears remarkably relaxed for someone delivering extensive lunch and dinner menus. This could reflect the laid-back spirit of Oaxaca, or may be thanks to the enlightened twins who own the restaurant. Whatever the reason, Miguel is quietly confident about his job, although surprisingly he started off in hydraulic engineering. "Little by little, cooking has taken me over," he admits. "To begin with it wasn't that important. But if you like eating, you like cooking. They go together, and now I couldn't imagine doing anything else."

The menu is a feast of Oaxacan ingredients updated and refreshed by the founding chef, Gabriel O'Farill. That means you can eat grasshopper and zucchini blossom crêpes or ants' eggs (harvested from the maguey plant) with butter, wormseed, and chili, while succulent corn fungus, *huitlacoche*, appears again and again. Miguel does, however, break out of the mold. "I'm free to invent dishes. For example, I make tuna

with pumpkin seeds or a fish carpaccio with ground coffee, chili, and orange sauce."

Much of his inspiration comes from his wife's birthplace, Tehuantepec. This eccentric town on the south coast of the state of Oaxaca is renowned not only for strong-minded Zapotec women but also for an addiction to partying. "Whenever we go there with our two children we end up in huge gatherings where people really concentrate on their food and drink," he laughs. "I've picked up great ideas there – like a thick shrimp soup made with onion, garlic, tomatoes, and two types of chili."

Miguel's knowledge is resolutely Mexican. "I love living here," he continues. "There's a better quality of life and far less stress than in Mexico City. I can also get very fresh ingredients from local farmers and I always find something new at the Central de Abastos. But the original Danzantes were about communication between the gods and human beings. I believe you need to feed the spirit and soul before the body." With that philosophical comment, Miguel returns behind the bar that separates the two visible worlds of this spiritually oriented restaurant; those of cooking and eating.

linguini with octopus, wild mushrooms, and smoked chili
linguini con pulpo y hongos silvestres

Pasta aficionados may be taken aback at the idea of reheating linguini, but the balance of flavors and textures is extraordinary – ever come across *mezcal* fighting for supremacy with chili before? Just go with the flow!

Cook the linguini in plenty of boiling water with the onion, garlic, *fines herbes*, oil, and a pinch of salt for about 10 minutes or until just tender. Drain, remove the onion, and set aside.

While the pasta is cooking, make the sauce. Heat the olive oil in a frying pan, add the octopus and wild mushrooms, and sauté until the mushrooms are tender.

In a blender or food processor, purée the chilies and garlic. Add to the octopus mixture in the frying pan.

Stir in the white wine and the *mezcal*, then add the linguini, toss well, and heat through. Season with salt and pepper, then serve immediately.

serves 6

1lb 9oz (700g) linguini

1 onion, peeled

1 garlic clove, peeled and crushed

1 tsp dried *fines herbes*

2 tsp vegetable oil

salt, to taste

for the sauce

3½fl oz (100ml) olive oil

1lb 12oz (800g) cooked octopus, chopped

3½oz (100g) wild mushrooms (*tecomate* or porcini)

4 roasted *pasilla* chilies, seeded and deveined

2 garlic cloves, peeled

5fl oz (150ml) white wine

2fl oz (50ml) *mezcal*

salt and freshly ground black pepper

swordfish carpaccio with soy and chili oil vinaigrette
carpaccio de pez vela con vinagreta de soya

Swordfish or tuna work equally well in this tender, slightly smoky-flavored carpaccio.

Place the fish in a shallow, non-metallic dish, pour over the orange juice, and leave to marinate for 2 hours.

Remove the fish from the marinade. Mix together the ground coffee and sesame seeds and press this mixture into the fish, covering it completely.

Briefly sear the coated fish to seal in the juices – about 30 seconds on each side. Then place in the freezer for about 15 minutes to firm up.

To make the citrus dressing, mix all the ingredients together in a bowl.

Cut the fish into very thin slices and arrange on a platter. Serve with shredded lettuce, a sprinkling of chives, and drizzle over the citrus dressing.

serves 6

3lb 5oz (1.5kg) swordfish or tuna filets, in three equal pieces

1¾ pints (1 liter) fresh orange juice

8oz (225g) ground coffee

3½ oz (100g) sesame seeds, toasted

1 small oakleaf lettuce, roughly shredded

handful of fresh chives, chopped

for the citrus dressing

18fl oz (500ml) fresh orange juice

3½ fl oz (100ml) fresh lemon juice

3½ fl oz (100ml) soy sauce

grilled tuna in shrimp, pumpkin seed, and *morita* chili sauce
atún en salsa de chile morita y camarón

The *morita* chili, despite its size, is a fiery one so you may want to reduce the quantity.

In a frying pan, toast the pumpkin seeds, then add the shrimp, *morita* chilies, *hoja de aguacate*, and garlic. Add 1 pint (600ml) of water and cook for 5 minutes. Remove from the heat and pour into a food processor. Blend until smooth and strain.

Heat the oil in a frying pan and add the chili sauce. Stir and heat through. Season with salt.

Grill or broil the tuna filets until cooked to your preference. Transfer to a serving plate and pour over the *morita* chili sauce.

serves 6

2lb 12oz (1.25 kg) fresh tuna, cut into 6 filets, about 7oz (200g) each

for the morita chili sauce

3½ oz (100g) pumpkin seeds

2oz (55g) dried shrimp

3 *morita* chilies

5 *hoja de aguacate* (Mexican or Haas avocado leaves)

2 garlic cloves, peeled and crushed

3 tbsp olive oil

salt, to taste

marinated poussin with *achiote* and onions
pollito de leche curado con achiote y cebollitas

This dish needs to be prepared the day before. The orange mixed with woody *achiote* marinade gives a very special kick, which is more typical of the Yucatán than Oaxaca.

Heat the oil in a saucepan, add the onion, garlic, *guajillo* chilies, and tomatoes and fry until the onion is softened. Pour in 7fl oz (200ml) of water, bring to a boil, reduce the heat, and simmer for 15 minutes.

Pour the chili mixture into a food processor, add the *achiote* paste and orange juice, and blend until smooth. Leave to cool.

Place the poussin halves in a non-metallic dish and pour over the cooled chili mixture. Cover and marinate in the refrigerator for 24 hours.

Place the onion rings in a dish. Mix together the remaining ingredients and pour over the onions. Cover and leave to marinate for at least 1 hour.

To cook the poussins, preheat the oven to 350ºF/180ºC. Arrange the poussin halves on a baking tray and roast, uncovered, for 40–50 minutes, or until cooked, turning over halfway through.

Serve with the marinated onion rings and some sautéed potatoes.

serves 6

1 tbsp vegetable oil

1 onion, peeled and roughly chopped

1 garlic clove, peeled and crushed

1¾oz (50g) *guajillo* chilies, seeded and deveined

1lb 2oz (500g) tomatoes, chopped

1¾oz (50g) *achiote* paste

1 pint (600ml) fresh orange juice

3 poussins, cut in half

for the marinated onion rings

1 red onion, peeled and cut into rings

2fl oz (50ml) vinegar

3½fl oz (100ml) fresh orange juice

1 tsp chopped fresh oregano

1 green chili, finely chopped

tacos with shredded duck and orange
tacos con chilorio de pato

Tacos are especially good at Los Danzantes. At certain times of the year they make them with *guisanos de maguey* – that's the maguey plant worm, a crunchy Oaxacan delicacy that also finds its way into bottles of *mezcal*. This piquant recipe uses orange to allay the strong chili and garlic flavors.

In a frying pan, heat the oil, and sauté the onion, garlic, and chilies until softened. Add the tomatoes and oregano and cook gently for about 15 minutes, stirring from time to time. Transfer to a food processor and blend to a purée.

Pour into a saucepan, stir in the vinegar and orange juice, and warm over low heat. Mix in the shredded duck meat, season with salt and pepper, and simmer for about 10 minutes.

Heat the *tortillas* on a griddle or in the oven (they should stay soft, not crisp). Place a tablespoonful or two of the duck mixture along the center of each, and fold in the sides to close. Serve garnished with avocado slices.

serves 6

2fl oz (50ml) vegetable oil

3 large onions, peeled and roughly chopped

3 garlic cloves, peeled and roughly chopped

5½oz (150g) *pasilla* chilies, roughly chopped

2 medium tomatoes, halved

1 tbsp Mexican orégano (or sage mixed with Italian oregano)

3½fl oz (100ml) white wine vinegar

10fl oz (300ml) fresh orange juice

salt and freshly ground black pepper

1 cooked duck, meat shredded

12 soft corn *tortillas*

2 large avocados, peeled, pitted, and sliced, to garnish

orange mousse with *mezcal*
mousse de naranja y mezcal

Whisk the egg whites until stiff, then gradually whisk in the sugar, one tablespoon at a time, to form a thick white meringue and set aside.

Whip the cream, adding the *mezcal*, until it just holds soft peaks, then gently fold in the meringue.

Pour all but three tablespoons of the orange juice into a saucepan and heat until nearly boiling, then take off the heat. Soak the gelatin in the remaining orange juice, then dissolve into the hot orange juice and leave to cool at room temperature.

Strain the orange jelly to remove any lumps and fold it gently into the whipped cream and meringue mixture. Pour into a glass dish and refrigerate for at least 4 hours or until set.

serves 4–6

7 large egg whites
14oz (400g) superfine sugar
16fl oz (450ml) whipping cream
3 tbsp *mezcal* or tequila
1 pint (600 ml) fresh orange juice
1oz (25g) powdered gelatin

Miguel makes this mousse with mangoes when they are in season as Mexican varieties are particularly sweet and juicy. Orange is a reliable substitute. If preferred, you can use tequila instead of *mezcal*, though no self-respecting Oaxaqueño would do that. Miguel serves his mousse trickled with a reduction of red wine, simmered with sugar.

market food

abigail mendoza's *xocolate con atole*

Abigail Mendoza is unforgettable. Diminutive, buxom, and energetic, with tiny hands and a huge personality, she really knows how to cook. A true Zapotec, with gold filigree earrings and a *shlappa* (braided satin ribbon) in her hair, she lives with her mother, six sisters, and four brothers in Teotitlán del Valle, the famous weaving village of the Oaxaca Valley. Inside the rambling family home is the Mendoza women's rug workshop and an informal restaurant called Tlamanalli, Zapotec for "gods of food."

"For the indigenous people, eating is sacred," explains Abigail. "And we Zapotecs really love food. When we have big fiestas we spend days preparing huge meals." Her expressive eyes widen. "I'm really proud that people love my food. A few years ago I was even invited to Paris to an Oaxacan food festival where I demonstrated corn-grinding on a *metate* (a lava stone grinding surface). I've been preparing corn and cooking since I was six. It was my father's idea to open a small restaurant; that was in 1990, before he died. He also taught me to weave and make vegetable dyes, and in turn I taught my sisters."

Abigail's conversation is punctuated with a melodic "Ah-hah!" and peals of laughter. Occasionally she turns to a younger sister to translate a Zapotec word into Spanish. As the unmarried eldest sister, she obviously feels responsible for Rosario, Marcelina, and Rufina, her sibling restaurant helpers. With two nieces also being introduced to the arts of the kitchen, the Mendoza dynasty is shaping up well for the future.

All Abigail's recipes are traditional and some, like her *Ndaushtilli* (chicken with corn, tomato, chili, and *hoja santa*), are specific to Teotitlán. Then there is her fabulous *xocolate con atole*, or *champurrado*. Derived from two Nahuatl words, *xoco* (bitter) and *atl* (water), it comes very close to the drink considered sacred by Moctezuma, the last Aztec emperor. In those days, after fermentation, the roasted and ground cocoa nibs were mashed with water, maize, *achiote* (sweet, peppery seeds), and chili. Today the solid chocolate contains varying amounts of cocoa bean, cinnamon, sugar (sometimes not), and almonds. Many people make their own or specify their favorite blend at a chocolate-milling shop.

Champurrado needs energetic preparation, starting with the solid chocolate, broken into pieces. For this, Abigail works on a *metate* with a *mano* (stone roller). Wetting both, she crushes the pieces with the roller, gradually diluting the chocolate with repeated "watering." Once a runny paste is obtained, she scrapes this into a deep clay bowl and whisks it with a *molinillo* (a wooden whisk), rubbing it between her hands to spin the liquid. Using this highly effective, ancient technique, the chocolate foam builds up rapidly into a bubbly cloud, light and frothy as air. The other stage is the *atole*, a thick porridge made by simmering maize flour with cinnamon, muscovado sugar, and water. When ready, the hot *atole* is poured into a large clay bowl and the chocolate foam spooned on top. You could call the result pre-Hispanic *nueva cocina* as the mixture has the contrasting temperatures (hot and cold) and textures (thick porridge and light foam) that are typical of this style of cooking.

Between weaving and cooking sessions, Abigail takes a break to sit at a table by the vividly tiled kitchen range where she chats and laughs with her mother and sisters. Her traditional Zapotec path seems harmonious, though she and her family have had the nous to open their doors to the outside world. Even more, Abigail's energy, humor, and extrovert nature have transformed her into the Zapotec Kitchen Diva.

zapotec blancmange
nicuatole

Abigail's party dessert is made with flour from a very specific local corn. There is a touch of Italian *pannacotta* about its texture. The cochineal coloring she uses is the real thing, made from little beetles, the source of Europe's cardinal red dye way back in the 16th-century.

In a large saucepan, mix 1¼ pints (700ml) of water with the milk, sugar, and cinnamon. Slowly bring to a boil then add the *masa harina*, stirring continuously to blend thoroughly. Cook gently for about 1 hour over low heat until thickened.

Pour two-thirds of the mixture into a deep, square serving dish. Mix a few drops of the coloring into the remaining mixture and pour on top. Cool and leave to set in the refrigerator, then cut into squares that will be part white, part pink. Serve in glass dishes.

serves 6–8

1¼ pints (700ml) whole milk

7oz (200g) muscovado sugar

2 cinnamon sticks

7oz (200g) *masa harina* (Mexican corn flour)

cochineal or red food coloring

yucatán

For many, the Yucatán has the most delectable food of all Mexico: an unexpected but winning mix of Mayan, Spanish, Middle Eastern, and Caribbean influences. It also marks a shift away from chili-mania towards red *achiote*, green pumpkin seeds, and citrus marinades. This is where meat (traditionally venison, turkey, duck, and wild boar) is cooked in a *pib* (a stone-lined pit used as an oven), where limes are tossed in with abandon, where *recados* (seasoned pastes) replace *moles,* and where one of the world's hottest chilies (the *habanero*) hails from. Behind it all is an indigenous culture that for nearly 3,000 years has dominated much of Central America. With their flat foreheads, high cheekbones, and noble noses, the Mayas are instantly recognizable. Yet not even their prodigious powers of prediction could have foretold the eclectic cuisine that was to take shape in the Yucatán.

Despite the mysterious and sudden decline of Ancient Maya 500 years earlier, the Spanish conquistadors met a population of resilient farmers who put up strong resistance. After a long, vicious campaign, the Mayas were forced to bow to a social structure that amounted to their enslavement. With their labor on the huge haciendas, immense fortunes were made from agriculture and then from the 19th-century sisal boom, which brought in French investment and cultural influence. In the late 19th-century, Lebanese and Syrian immigrants also entered the cultural melting pot. These talented traders generated more wealth – and a passion for Ottoman cuisine. For Mayan workers, a semblance of equality only emerged after the 1910 Revolution. The Yucatán has hardly looked back since.

Jutting out into the Gulf of Mexico, the peninsula was always geographically isolated from the rest of the country, resulting in stronger trade links with the Caribbean and Europe. Even today, the Yucatán's distinctive *mestizo* (mixed race) culture sometimes echoes Cuba, just across the water, far more than Mexico. Economically, too, it is separate, and the enviable standard of living and sense of security are attracting more and more well-to-do Mexicans from the north. Mérida is their chief destination: a lively city with elegance, atmosphere, and vermilion flame-trees as well as a sticky tropical climate occasionally alleviated by torrential rains. In the 19th-century, French investment spawned a kind of Champs Elysées, the Paseo de Montejo, lined with ornately stuccoed *belle époque* mansions. This avenue now the marks the borderline between old and new Mérida, between streets of vividly colored colonial houses, churches, and little plazas on one side and the burgeoning modern suburbs on the other, where shopping-malls, walled residences, and SUVs rule.

Beyond the city unfolds another, more evocative world: one of towering ceiba trees, sleepy dogs and darting lizards, thatched Mayan huts, gently swinging hammocks, and crumbling haciendas. Most of the flat peninsula is blanketed in low jungle and savannah. The only bumps on the horizon are the Puuc Hills, just south of Mérida, where several Mayan sites are located, above all magnificent Uxmal with its elliptical Pyramid of the Magician. Chichen Itza, the largest, most famous Mayan site, lies east of Mérida, while all over the peninsula countless structures lie shrouded in vegetation. Slowly, as highways are extended, villages are tidied up, and haciendas converted into hotels, that idiosyncratic time capsule begins to disappear.

Back in Mérida, there is nothing sleepy about the peninsula's largest market, sprawling over one city block. Business is brisk yet transactions civilized, with no hard sales pitch, just tiny Mayan women in traditional white *huipiles* (embroidered tunics) chatting amiably in a language peppered with x's, k's, and ch's and much clicking of tongues. In front are buckets of fragrant tuberoses and creamy arum lilies, mountains of ground pumpkin seeds, all the better to make the sauce for *papadzules* (Yucatecan *enchilada*), bright red *recado* packed with *achiote* seeds, black *recado* made from charred chilies, fat and fragrant allspice berries, banana leaves for *tamales* and for baking in the *pib*, local oregano, and a devilish little sauce called *salsa diablita* (little devil) thanks to its searing *habanero* content. Round the corner is the seafood section, packed with families eating seafood cocktails beside piles of fresh dogfish, snapper, and squid.

Fruit has always been big with the Mayas. Depending on the season, there are heaps of plums, large and small mangoes, *zapote mamey*, papaya, *chaya* (a local plant like young spinach), coconuts, avocados, and bitter oranges, widely used for marinades. Local *limas*, sometimes called "sweet limes" are neither lemon nor lime, as they are milder and more fragrant. Heady flavors come in recycled jars of wild honey and sweetness in bottles of *xtabentun*, a honeyed anise liqueur.

Just outside the market is the purveyor of the Yucatán's greatest anomaly: big, waxy red *queso de bola* – in other words, Edam cheese. Bizarrely, when stuffed with spicy meat and raisins, *queso relleno* (stuffed cheese) is the local hit. The origin? In the old days, after cargo-ships had delivered valuable sisal to Europe, they needed ballast to fill the empty holds for the return journey. What better than these waterproof, edible footballs? Thus was born yet another Yucatecan hybrid. With this impressive ability to absorb and transform, the region now occupies the top rung of Mexico's gastronomic ladder.

martiniano ek ayin
hacienda teya

The reputation of 17th-century Hacienda Teya is set in stone; quite literally, as it was the first hacienda in the Yucatán peninsula to be restored and converted into a hotel and restaurant. Today there are dozens, but Teya holds it own thanks to its delicious, authentic Yucatecan cuisine. As well as serving leisurely lunches to the well-heeled every day, the restaurant is *the* place for any large-scale celebration in the Mérida area. Even Hillary Clinton has graced the rambling mansion with a visit.

Maintaining such a high profile is demanding, but Veronica Cárdenas, daughter of the founder, has boundless energy. "My father had the vision when he bought the hacienda 32 years ago in a fit of enthusiasm," she recounts. "The rest of our family were worried about the scale of it but as he'd owned a Yucatecan restaurant in Mexico City, he knew his stuff. Then he started collecting recipes from friends and relatives but was careful to limit the menu. Like him, I believe quality is in inverse proportion to the number of dishes on offer."

Right from the start, the kitchen has been headed by Martiniano Ek Ayin, a 55-year-old with such expressive Mayan features that his eyebrows occasionally hit the rim of his tall chef's toque. With a winning smile edged by shyness, he recalls his early days. "Before I learned to cook I was a tailor but in the tiny village where I lived there wasn't much work. So I took a cooking course and started working in various restaurants in Mérida – even a Chinese one!" With evident pleasure he adds,

"Now I only ever cook Yucatecan specialities. The dish I am most proud of is my *cochinita pibil*. It needs a day of marinating to get rid of the fat, then three hours of cooking." As he talks, Martiniano's eyes sparkle and communicate real passion, pouring straight from the heart into the cooking pot.

In the huge garden outside the restaurant, tropical birds whoop and whistle and gusts of wind rustle the crimson bougainvillea. Martiniano shows off the different types of orange trees that produce essential ingredients for his dishes. "I love this garden as I don't have one myself. I live nearby in the village with my second wife and our son. Right by the fourth *tope* [speed-bump]!" he chuckles.

Ask him for an alternative to the ubiquitous banana leaf, so often used in Yucatecan *tamales* and other dishes, and Martiniano suggests a kind of oak leaf. "Or any other leaf which gives flavor," he adds, beaming engagingly. Here, in such lush, tropical surroundings, it must be difficult to imagine countries without banana leaves or other outsized equivalents. Martiniano manages, just, as he adds, "Okay, you can use silver foil if you like." Even the Yucatán eventually moves on.

cream of cilantro soup
crema de cilantro

Creamy, subtle, and pungent, this is a great new take on vegetable soup. It can be served with croutons.

Melt the butter in a large saucepan and sweat the garlic, onion, and vegetables over a low heat until softened. Stir the flour into the juices and continue stirring while pouring in half of the milk and adding the bay leaves.

Stir the cilantro into the remaining milk and pour into the saucepan. Crumble in the bouillon cubes. Bring to a boil and simmer for 5 minutes until the soup thickens, then strain and serve immediately.

serves 6

8 tbsp butter

2 garlic cloves, peeled and finely chopped

1 onion, peeled and finely chopped

1 small green pepper, seeded and finely chopped

1 small leek, finely chopped

3 celery stalks, finely chopped

2 carrots, finely chopped

3 tbsp all-purpose flour

3¼ pints (2 liters) milk

3 bay leaves

3 small bunches of fresh cilantro, very finely chopped

2 chicken bouillon cubes

lime and chicken broth
sopa de lima

serves 6

1–2 skinned chicken breasts, about 10½oz (300g) in total

1 whole garlic bulb, peeled

1 sprig of fresh oregano

small bunch of fresh cilantro

salt, to taste

2 tbsp corn oil

1lb (450g) onions, peeled and roughly chopped

14oz (400g) green peppers, seeded and chopped

7oz (200g) tomatoes, chopped

juice of 6 limes

2 chicken bouillon cubes

4 soft corn *tortillas*, cut in thin strips and lightly fried

2 limes, thinly sliced

Pour 3¼ pints (2 liters) of water into a large saucepan and add the chicken breasts, garlic, oregano, and cilantro and salt. Bring to a boil over high heat then turn the heat down to low–medium and simmer for about 30 minutes or until the chicken is cooked.

Remove the chicken from the broth, shred, and set aside. Strain the broth and set aside.

Heat the oil in a large saucepan and sauté the onions, peppers, and tomatoes over low heat until softened. Then pour in the strained chicken broth, add the lime juice, and crumble in the bouillon cubes. Simmer for 10 minutes, then strain the broth again.

To serve, place some shredded chicken, a few *tortilla* strips, and a slice or two of lime in individual serving bowls, then pour over the hot chicken broth.

It is virtually impossible not to become hooked on this divine, piquant broth, an absolute classic of the Yucatán peninsula that has now traveled far afield. Martiniano's version is one of the best.

chicken with capers
pollo alcaparrado

Native to the Yucatán, the *x'catik,* or *güero,* chili pepper is long, lime green, and very hot. If necessary, replace it with *habanero* but beware – either is pure fire! Otherwise, milder chilies will do. Here, the typically Yucatecan flavor of sour orange is countered by sweet raisins and sharp capers. It is quite delicious and an easy main course to serve for a dinner party.

Joint the chicken into two breasts and two legs and place in a non-metallic dish.

Whiz half the capers and the orange juice in a blender or food processor. Add half the roasted garlic and season to taste with salt, pepper, and boullion powder.

Pour over the chicken, cover, and marinate in the refrigerator for at least 1 hour or up to 24 hours.

Heat the oil in a large saucepan. Remove the chicken pieces from the marinade, saving the liquid to use later. Pat the chicken dry with paper towels and fry until golden brown all over.

To the saucepan add 1¾ pints (1 liter) of water, the marinade, and the roasted chili, taking care not to break it open. Stir in the remaining capers, the olives, and raisins and simmer, covered, for 10 minutes.

Add the potatoes, onion, and the remaining garlic. Simmer, covered, for about 20 minutes or until the potatoes and chicken are cooked.

Divide the chicken pieces between four bowls and serve with the potatoes and a ladle or two of broth.

serves 4

1 chicken, about 2lb 4oz (1kg)

2oz (55g) capers

juice of 5 peeled, bitter oranges
   such as Seville

2–3 garlic cloves, peeled and roasted

salt and freshly ground black pepper

1 tsp chicken boullion powder

2 tbsp vegetable oil

1 *x'catik* (*güero*) chili, roasted

1oz (25g) pitted green olives

1 tbsp seedless raisins

7oz (200g) potatoes, peeled
   and quartered

1 onion, peeled, quartered,
   and roasted

slow-baked pork
cochinita pibil

To make the *frijoles refritos* bring 5¼ pints (3 liters) of water to a boil in a large saucepan. Drain the soaking water from the beans and add them to the saucepan with the parsley and garlic. Cover the saucepan with a lid and simmer over medium heat for 2½–3 hours until the beans are tender. Add a pinch of salt as the beans begin to split open. Purée the cooked beans in a blender or food processor.

Heat the oil in a large saucepan, add the onion and the whole chili pepper, and sauté until the onion is golden. Add the puréed beans and simmer gently over a low heat, stirring continuously, until the mixture thickens.

To make the *achiote* paste, put all the ingredients, except the vinegar or orange juice, in a food processor. Whiz to mix well, then, little by little, add just enough vinegar or orange juice to create a thick paste.

Season the pork with the salt and pepper and rub over the garlic.

Whisk the *achiote* paste into the orange juice and pour the mixture over the meat. Cover and leave to marinate in the refrigerator for at least 1 hour, or longer if possible (the longer, the better).

Preheat the oven to 400°C/200°C.

Place a banana leaf or a sheet of aluminum foil on the bottom of a baking dish, put the pork on top, sprinkle with oregano, then cover with the other banana leaf or another sheet of foil. Cover the dish tightly with a lid or with aluminum foil to prevent the steam from escaping and bake for about 1 hour or until the pork is cooked through.

To prepare the marinated red onion, briefly blanch the onion in boiling water, then immediately douse in cold water and drain. Put in a non-metallic dish, pour over the orange juice, season with salt, and set aside for about 1 hour.

Serve the pork with the *frijoles refritos* and marinated red onion.

serves 8

2lb 4oz (1kg) boned shoulder or leg of pork, cut into bite-sized pieces

salt and freshly ground black pepper

2 garlic cloves, peeled and crushed

1 pint (600ml) fresh bitter orange juice, such as Seville

2 banana leaves or aluminum foil

2–3 tsp chopped fresh oregano

for the frijoles refritos (refried black beans)

1lb 2oz (500g) black beans, cleaned and soaked overnight in water

small bunch fresh flat-leaf parsley

1 garlic clove, peeled

2 tbsp sunflower oil

1 onion, peeled and finely chopped

1 x'catik (güero) chili

for the achiote paste marinade

4 tbsp *achiote* seeds

1 tbsp chopped fresh oregano

1 tbsp cumin seeds

1½ tsp coarsely ground black pepper

12 peppercorns

10 garlic cloves, peeled

white wine vinegar or bitter orange juice

for the marinated red onion

14oz (400g) red onions, peeled and chopped

juice of 3 peeled, bitter oranges such as Seville

salt, to taste

Sadly, very little pork is still cooked in a *pib*, a stone-lined underground fire pit used for baking since the days of the ancient Maya. Today, urban families and most restaurants have opted for a conventional oven, which cannot replicate the smoky, crisp finish of a traditional fire pit. But this tender, marinated pork is still a feast when served with the marinated red onions and *frijoles refritos*.

grilled pork in orange marinade
poc chuc

At Hacienda Teya they serve this divine pork dish with hot corn *tortillas* and fiery *habanero* chilies. The sourness of the bitter orange works wonderfully with the pork, particularly when it is grilled over hot charcoal on a barbecue. Don't skip the side dishes, as they really complete the picture.

To make the *frijoles*, bring 2¼ pints (1½ liters) of water to a boil in a large saucepan. Drain the soaking water from the beans and add them to the saucepan with the *epazote* and garlic. Cover the saucepan with a lid and simmer over medium heat for 2½–3 hours or until the beans are tender. Add salt when the beans begin to split open.

Season the pork filet with salt and pepper and rub over the garlic. Cut into slices about ½in (1cm) thick. Arrange in a non-metallic dish and pour over the bitter orange juice. Cover and leave to stand for 1 hour.

To prepare the marinated onions, grill the whole onions on a hot griddle or under a broiler, turning frequently until lightly browned all over. Leave to cool then peel and cut into ½in (1cm) pieces. Mix the onion with the bitter orange juice, cilantro, and salt, and set aside for about 1 hour.

To make the *chiltomate*, roast the tomatoes on a hot griddle or under a broiler, turning frequently, then mash. Add the chopped onion, cilantro, and salt and set aside in the refrigerator.

Drain the cooked beans, tip them into a food processor, and whiz to a purée. Heat the oil in a large saucepan, add the onion and the whole chili, and sauté until the onion is golden. Add the bean purée and a sprig of *epazote*. Bring to a boil and simmer for about 5 minutes, then strain through a sieve.

Grill the pork filets on a hot griddle, under a broiler, or over hot charcoal for about 4–5 minutes on each side or until just cooked.

Serve the filets with the marinated red onion, *chiltomate*, and *frijoles*. Garnish with orange wedges.

serves 6

2lb (900g) pork filet

salt and freshly ground black pepper

1–2 garlic cloves, peeled and finely chopped

juice of 2 bitter oranges, such as Seville

2 bitter oranges, such as Seville, cut into quarters, to garnish

for the frijoles (black beans)

9oz (250g) black beans, cleaned and soaked overnight

1 handful of fresh *epazote*

1 small garlic clove, peeled and crushed

salt, to taste

1 tbsp vegetable oil

1 small onion, peeled and chopped

1 *x'catik* chili

for the marinated red onion

14oz (400g) red onions

juice from 3 bitter oranges, such as Seville

bunch fresh cilantro, chopped

salt, to taste

for the chiltomate (salsa)

1lb 2oz (500g) tomatoes

1 small onion, peeled and finely chopped

small bunch of fresh cilantro, finely chopped

salt, to taste

marinated turkey in spicy onion broth
pavo en escabeche oriental

You need to set aside an afternoon to prepare this, to allow for the marinating and the cooking time. It appears deceptively simple when cooked, however, and is usually served with white rice and *frijoles refritos*.

Clean and season the turkey, joint into two breasts and two legs, and place in a non-metallic dish.

To make the *escabeche*, grind all the ingredients, except the salt and vinegar or orange juice, together using a pestle and mortar and then sieve. Blend in the vinegar or orange juice to form a thick paste. Season with salt.

Stir 3½oz (100g) of the *escabeche* into the 1 pint (600ml) of bitter orange juice. Pour over the turkey joints and marinate for at least 2 hours.

Transfer the turkey and marinade to a large saucepan, pour in 1¾ pints (1 liter) of water and bring to a boil over high heat. Reduce the heat to medium, cover with a lid, and simmer for 2 hours.

Remove from the heat and leave to cool a little before lifting the turkey out of the saucepan. Cut or shred the turkey meat into small pieces. Strain the stock.

In a deep saucepan, heat the olive oil and sweat the onions and garlic over low heat until softened. Add the chilies and turkey stock and bring to a boil. Stir in the shredded turkey, heat through, and serve.

serves 6–8

1 turkey, about 9lb 3oz (4kg)

1 pint (600ml) fresh bitter orange juice, such as Seville

salt, to taste

2 tbsp olive oil

1lb 2oz (500g) onions, peeled and cut into strips

2–3 garlic cloves, peeled and crushed

5 *x'catik* (*güero*) chilies, roasted and chopped, or yellow cayenne pepper

for the escabeche (pickling sauce)

4 black peppercorns

5 cloves

1½ tsp freshly ground black pepper

½ tsp dried oregano

½ tsp cumin

5 garlic cloves, peeled

1½ tsp white wine vinegar or bitter orange juice

salt, to taste

shredded venison
tzic de venado

Deer used to be common in the Yucatán so venison crops up in many traditional recipes. This one is a light, chilled dish, ideal for lunch on a hot, sultry day. Serve on a wide platter with slices of avocado, tomato, lettuce, and slivers of *habanero* chilies. *Frijoles* and warm *tortillas* are also classic accompaniments.

Preheat the oven to 350°F/180°C. Season the venison with salt, pepper, and oregano and wrap in banana leaves or aluminum foil. Place in a roasting pan, cover with foil, and bake for about 15 minutes until the meat has dried.

Remove from the oven, unwrap, and shred finely.

In a large bowl, mix the shredded venison with the radishes, cilantro, and onion. Stir in the orange juice and season with salt. Refrigerate until cold.

Serve garnished with orange segments.

serves 4–6

2lb 4oz (1kg) cooked venison
   (or beef), thickly sliced

salt and freshly ground black pepper

1 tsp dried oregano

banana leaves or aluminum foil

large bunch of radishes,
   finely sliced

large bunch of fresh cilantro,
   finely chopped

1 small onion, peeled and
   finely chopped

juice of 4 bitter oranges

1–2 bitter oranges, such as Seville,
   peeled and segmented, to garnish

candied papaya and cheese
dulce de papaya con queso

Cubes of glistening orange papaya and smooth Edam cheese unite here in a simple yet sumptuous dessert. The caustic lime (calcium hydroxide) is essential to prevent the fruit from disintegrating during cooking. (It is not the same as calcium oxide (quicklime) which is very dangerous.) Be very careful to rinse the fruit thoroughly afterwards.

Cut the papaya lengthwise into slices about 1½in (4cm) thick, then cut the slices into bite-sized cubes.

Stir the caustic lime into 18fl oz (500ml) of water and soak the papaya in this mixture for about 1 hour. There should be enough water to cover the fruit.

Rinse the fruit in lots of cold running water and place in a saucepan. Add 9fl oz (250ml) of water together with the sugar, vanilla, and cinnamon. Cover with a lid and simmer over low heat without stirring for 1½ hours. Remove from the heat and leave to cool before refrigerating.

Serve chilled, tossed with the cubes of cheese.

serves 4

3lb 5oz (1.5 kg) papaya, peeled and seeds removed

4 tbsp caustic lime (pickling lime)

2lb 4oz (1kg) superfine sugar

1 tbsp vanilla extract

1 cinnamon stick

2oz (55g) Edam cheese (or any smooth, mild cheese), diced

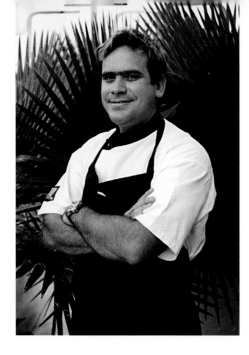

roberto solis
nectar

All the Yucatecan clichés fly out the window when you arrive at Nectar, a funkily designed restaurant opened by Roberto Solis and his business partner, Santiago Pineda Leyva, in 2004. There is icy white furniture, designer tableware, a calming aquarium, a superlative wine-list, and chatty young waiters sporting long maroon aprons and spiky hair thick with gel. Located in a residential suburb of Mérida, Nectar appeals to affluent young things eager to enjoy a reinvention of flavors and first-class presentation.

Roberto is a young chef with attitude and an infectious laugh. Laid back, with a mischievous smile and brimming with confidence, he would bond with any cool urban gathering on the globe. His fluent English has an American twang as, although a native of Mérida, this 30-year-old is well-traveled. He readily admits to having been the black sheep of his family. Not any longer though, as business is booming and he hopes that the success of Nectar will be followed by an equally popular *antojítos* (Mexican tapas) bar just around the corner.

Although the hard work is done by the tall, reserved Santiago in the management department and by a brilliant and very focused young head of kitchen, Gaspard Tamayo, the recipes are mainly Roberto's own. "I got to like food when I started working at the Cajun Grill," Roberto jokes. "Then I realized that something was missing in Mérida so I did an apprenticeship in catering. My nanny always cooked typical Yucatecan food but sadly that's being lost now. American influences are changing attitudes here."

Roberto's own perception of cooking blossomed in an unexpected place: Denmark. For three months he worked side by side with René Redzepi, the young Macedonian chef whose restaurant, Noma, has put Copenhagen on the gastro map. "That's where I developed my liking for oats – they're wonderful!" Roberto enthuses as he proffers a *relleno negro* (a spicy, chili-based black stuffing) made with crunchy oats, an ingredient that is unheard of in the Yucatán. He also worked briefly with Heston Blumenthal at *The Fat Duck,* so "molecular cuisine" is not new to him.

"In my opinion there's only one chef working in a unique way in Mexico, and that's Enrique Olvera in Mexico City," he states. "What we really need to do in Mexico is get together and work on our standards. The ingredients are so fantastic here, we can cook anything! We need to raise the bar while sticking to local produce." And his favorite ingredient? "It's corn!" he grins. "You can do so much with it – it's incredibly versatile." Despite that international veneer, Roberto's heart could not be more Mexican.

Relleno negro is a black chili sauce flavored with burnt chilies and spices, usually served with turkey in a broth. *Nectar's* original use of this Yucatecan classic is really something else, especially when combined with crunchy oats and a creamy poached egg. If you are going to cook only one Nectar recipe, then this should be it.

oats in black chili sauce
avena en relleno negro

To make the *relleno negro*, wash the chilies, remove the seeds and veins, and then grill on a griddle or under a broiler until well charred.

Blend the chilies, garlic, *epazote,* and salt in a food processor or blender and add just enough water to achieve a fairly thick paste.

In a deep saucepan, whisk the black chili sauce into the chicken stock and warm over medium heat.

Stir in the oats and cook over medium heat, stirring from time to time, for about 5 minutes or until the liquid is absorbed and the oats are cooked but still separate. Add salt and pepper to taste.

In a frying pan, heat the garlic oil and sauté the bacon and snails. Set aside.

Fry the reserved bacon rind until crisp. Allow to cool then crush into crumbs.

Poach the eggs in water at 113°F/45°C for 30 minutes.

To serve, place a large tablespoon of oat mixture in the center of each bowl. Top with a poached egg, and arrange the fried bacon and snails around it. Sprinkle over some diced avocado, crumbs of crunchy bacon rind, and cilantro leaves. Garnish with a few flowers. Serve immediately.

serves 4

1½ pints (1 liter) chicken stock

10¾oz (300g) rolled oats

salt and freshly ground black pepper

3 tbsp garlic-flavored oil

7oz (200g) thickly sliced Canadian bacon cut into small pieces, rind removed and saved

5oz (140g) snails, shelled (frozen or canned are fine)

4 eggs

1 avocado, peeled, pitted, and cut into small cubes

small bunch of fresh cilantro leaves

a handful of colorful, edible flowers, such as nasturtiums, to garnish (optional)

for the relleno negro
(black chili sauce)

9oz (250g) dried red chilies

4 large garlic cloves

2 bunches of fresh *epazote* or tarragon

salt, to taste

crab and avocado ravioli
raviolis de cangrejo y aguacate

This makes a spectacularly pretty sculpture, perfectly balanced in flavor, texture, and color. It needs careful though not difficult preparation and should be assembled just before serving. Using white bowls will set off the colors beautifully.

To prepare the filling, heat the oil in a frying pan and sauté the crab meat, carrot, and garlic. When the carrot is tender, stir in the parsley, and season with salt and pepper. Set aside to cool.

To make the ravioli, lay a sheet of lasagne flat on a chopping board. Put a heaped teaspoon of filling at each corner, leaving a good border of pasta around each. Brush the beaten egg between and around each mound of filling. Lay a second sheet of lasagne on top and press down firmly between the filling to seal. Divide the sheets into individual ravioli by running a pizza cutter or knife between the mounds. Repeat with the remaining pasta sheets and filling.

Bring a saucepan of lightly salted water to a rolling boil, drop in the ravioli and cook for 6–8 minutes until the pasta is tender.

To make the avocado purée, blitz all the ingredients with 2½fl oz (75ml) of water in a blender or food processor until smooth.

To whisk up the *achiote* foam, mix all the ingredients in a saucepan. Bring to a boil and boil for 1 minute. Cool slightly then use a hand-blender to whip the mixture into a foam.

To serve, spread a generous amount of avocado purée over the base of each white bowl. Stack four ravioli on top and crown with a spoonful of *achiote* foam.

serves 8 as an appetizer, 4 as a main course

16 sheets fresh lasagne

1 egg, beaten

for the crab filling

2 tbsp vegetable oil

1lb 2oz (500g) white crab meat, finely chopped

1 carrot, peeled and finely chopped

1 garlic clove, finely chopped

small bunch of flat-leaf parsley, finely chopped

salt and freshly ground black pepper

for the avocado purée

1–2 avocados, about 12oz (350g), peeled and pitted

4 tsp lime juice

1 tsp salt

for the achiote foam

18fl oz (500ml) chicken broth

2 tbsp lecithin powder (available from health food stores)

3oz (85g) *achiote* paste

1 tbsp chicken bouillon powder

salt, to taste

fried plantain wafers with venison
tostones con venado

Green plantains can be tough to peel; it helps to soak them in warm water for 15 minutes or so beforehand. Fried plantains are a Caribbean classic but in Roberto's inventive hands they become a highly sophisticated appetizer – both crisp and tender. You can replace the venison with shredded pork.

Place the shredded venison in a small bowl, sprinkle with a few drops of lemon juice, and lightly season with salt and pepper. Set aside.

Fry the plantain chunks in the oil until they are soft. Remove from the oil with a slotted spoon and lay on a paper towels to absorb any excess oil. Then flatten, one at a time, in a *tortilla* press, to form rounds. Alternatively, place each chunk in a plastic freezer bag, one at a time, and roll flat with a rolling pin or glass bottle until about ½inch (1cm) thick. Stamp out a regular circle with a straight-edged biscuit cutter.

Briefly fry the plantain wafers in the same oil for about 3 minutes, turning until golden brown on both sides.

Prepare the wafers immediately by topping each plantain disc with slices of tomato, radish, and avocado, then top with a spoonful of shredded venison. Garnish with a sprinkling of cilantro leaves.

serves 4 (2–3 *tostones* each)

7oz (200g) cooked shredded venison

juice of ½ lemon

salt and freshly ground black pepper

4 green plantains, peeled and cut into ¾–1¼in (2–3cm) chunks

4 tbsp vegetable oil

1–2 firm medium tomatoes, cut into 12 paper-thin slices

2–4 small radishes, cut into 12 paper-thin slices

1 avocado, peeled, pitted, and cut into 12 paper-thin slices

small bunch of cilantro leaves roughly chopped, to garnish

mango fruits
xec de mango

An intriguing mix of sweet tropical fruit with watery but crisp *jícama* and bitter orange granita makes a delectably fresh dessert – although Nectar serves this as a kind of *trou normand* between savory courses on their tasting menu. The cilantro and chili powder give a typically Mexican edge.

At least an hour before serving, mix the bitter orange juice with the sugar and 2 tablespoons of water, pour into an ice cube tray, and put in the freezer.

Place the *jícama* slices in water with plenty of ice and leave for about 5 minutes or until they curl up. Remove and drain on a paper towel.

Refresh the cilantro leaves in iced water, remove, and pat dry with paper towel. Chop roughly.

Remove the iced orange juice from the freezer and turn out from the ice cube tray. Arrange the ice cubes on a serving plate with the orange segments, *jícama* and mango, then sprinkle with the chili powder, salt, a few drops of lemon juice, and a sprinkling of cilantro. Serve immediately.

serves 4–6

8fl oz (225ml) bitter orange juice, such as Seville

1–2 tbsp superfine sugar

small bunch fresh cilantro leaves

4 oranges, peeled and divided into segments

½ *jícama* or 4 small juicy young turnips, thinly sliced

4 large ripe mangoes, peeled, pitted, and thinly sliced

chili powder, to taste

salt, to taste

juice of ½ lemon

market food

marcelino avila's *ceviche*

Looking for a lost time and place in the Yucatán? Then try Celestún, a tiny beach resort with a flamingo reserve attached. Due west of Mérida, it is reached by a long, straight road that slices through endless low jungle and scrub and the odd Mayan village. Finally, after crossing mangroves and a flamingo lagoon, the road ends abruptly at the beach. Here, a ramshackle line-up of *palapas* (thatched huts), modest restaurants, and concrete houses painted in wild colors from deep emerald to Gauloise blue overlook the white sand and tepid waters of the Gulf of Mexico. Dogs snooze in the shade; fishermen haul in their catch; coconuts dangle from palms; pelicans swoop; and boys kick balls around. Meanwhile the restaurants do a steady trade between local families and famished birdwatchers.

La Playita, one of the oldest and certainly the quaintest of the beach-cafés, offers a succulent *ceviche* made with freshwater shrimp, octopus, and crab, all caught locally. This is made by the owner's son, Marcelino Avila, whose eye make-up and nail polish are as carefully crafted as his ingredients. There is a Felliniesque

quality to the group of eccentric locals who gather here at the end of each day, from a Cuban exile who rowed to Miami and ended up in Celestún ("running a ½ star hotel") to an old man in a baseball hat who spends his time rearranging an eclectic collection of stuffed local fauna – armadillos, iguanas, anteaters, and alligators. In a corner, an altar is surmounted with a plastic statue of Christ surrounded with arum lilies. Above hangs a reproduction of Da Vinci's *The Last Supper* next to flaking murals of flamingos. As the sun sinks on the horizon, Pedro Avila, the owner, and Gilberto, the main waiter, start closing down the beachside area and piling up chairs. However remote Celustún may feel, Marcelino's exquisite *ceviches* will continue to pull in the crowds.

mixed seafood salad
ceviche mixto

This is the perfect dish to eat on a hot day with a chilled Mexican beer or two.

serves 6

7oz (200g) cooked fresh crab meat or any very fresh fish

juice of 2 limes

1 bay leaf

salt and freshly ground black pepper

7oz (200g) fresh shrimp, steamed for 5 minutes and shelled

7oz (200g) cooked octopus, chopped

1 plump tomato, diced

1 medium onion, peeled and finely chopped

½ avocado, peeled, pitted, and finely chopped

small bunch of fresh cilantro, finely chopped

chili powder, to taste

1 lime, cut into 6 wedges, to garnish

taco chips (optional)

Put the crab meat in a non-metallic dish and add the lime juice, bay leaf, and salt and pepper. Allow to marinate for 2–3 hours.

Mix the marinated crab, shrimp, octopus, tomato, onion, and avocado together in a large serving bowl. Stir in the cilantro and the lime juice marinade and season with salt, pepper, and chili powder to taste. Decorate with the lime wedges.

Serve slightly chilled with *taco* chips.

SELECT GLOSSARY

Achiote: annatto. Dark red seeds with woody flavor which produce scarlet coloring, popular in the Yucatán. A major part of *recado rojo.* Also comes as a paste.

Amaranto: amaranth. The seeds become a biscuit called *alegria* or are ground and added to corn flour and honey, or toasted and ground into gluten-free flour. High in protein, fiber, and iron. Amaranth seeds should always be cooked because they block digestive uptake when raw.

Antojítos: "little whims." Mexican tapas or appetizers. A vast, ever-shifting category, they change name with regions and minor variations in form or filling. Basically a corn "container" filled with delicious things, whether *taco, burrito, enchilada, chalupa, panucho, quesadilla,* or *papdzul.*

Ceviche: marinated fish. Raw fish or shellfish marinated in lime juice with chili, onion, garlic, and cilantro. Popular on the Pacific coast in Acapulco and the Gulf Coast in Veracruz and the Yucatán.

Chiles/Chilies: a digestive stimulant and an addiction, as they trigger endorphin "highs." Mexico grows around 150 types, from relatively mild *pasilla* and *ancho* to fiery *chipotle, cayenne,* and *habanero.* Usually the larger ones are milder. Most of the heat is in the veins and seeds, which are unaffected by cooking or freezing. Buy plump, unwrinkled specimens. The usual way to cook chilies is to roast them over a flame until the skin is charred, then seal in a paper or plastic bag for 15 minutes or so to sweat. Hold under running cold water and flake off the burnt skin. Beware: your skin and eyes can burn from chili juices so wash your hands after handling them. The best antidote is to soak your hands in milk or yogurt.

SCOVILLE SCALE

The more capsaicin, the fierier the chili. Capsaicin levels were first measured by Wilbur Lincoln Scoville (1865–1942), an American chemist who drew up a table of units. Below are the most commonly used Mexican chilies, though the world's hottest, *Naga Jolokia,* is Indian and shoots off the scale at over 1 million units.

BELL PEPPER	0
ANAHEIM	500 – 1,000
NEW MEXICO	500 – 1,000
ANCHO	1000 – 1500
MULATO	1000 – 1500
PASILLA	1000 – 1500
POBLANO	1000 – 1500
X'CATIC (GÜERO)	2500 – 5000
GUAJILLO	2500 – 5000
JALAPEÑO	2500 – 5000
SERRANO	10,000 – 23,000
ARBOL	15,000 – 30,000
CHIPOTLE	15,000 – 30,000
MORITA	15,000 – 30,000
CAYENNE (TABASCO)	30,000 – 50,000
PIQUIN	50,000 – 100,000
HABANERO	100,000 – 350,000

Elote: cooked or canned sweetcorn, or barbecued corn on the cob.

Epazote: wormseed. A strong aromatic wild herb often cooked with beans to reduce flatulence, also a remedy for intestinal disorders. Seeds and dried *epazote,* almost as good, are available by mail order. Mexicans swear by it.

Frijoles: beans. Mexico's 7,000-year-old legume can be red kidney, pinto (speckled brown, the *refritos* classic), black (the Mayan favorite, cooked with *epazote*), or yellow.

Frijoles refritos: boiled beans mashed and fried with *piquin* chili, a standard for *tortas* and *tacos* and with fried egg breakfasts. High in protein and carbohydrates and full of vitamins, minerals, and fiber. Only add salt at the end of cooking or it takes twice as long for the beans to soften.

Hoja de aguacate: avocado leaf. Fresh or dried, they are used in soups, stews, and with beans and can replace *hoja santa* in green *mole*.

Hoja santa/Hierba santa/Acuyo: a wonderful, anise-scented leaf often used for wrapping fish and *tamales,* and in green *mole*. Grows in south-central Mexico. Big, about 8–10in (20–25cm), with a very special flavor.

Huitlacoche/Cuitlacoche: corn truffle. A fungus that grows naturally on ears of corn and has an earthy, smoky flavor. A great delicacy, often cooked with garlic and chili for *tacos, tamales,* and *quesadillas.* No one should be put off by the Nahuatl name, which means "raven's excrement." Outside Mexico, canned *huitlacoche* is available.

Jícama: sometimes translated as yam bean or Mexican potato. This juicy tuber is similar to turnip and native to Mexico and California. The crisp, white flesh is eaten as a snack seasoned with chili pepper, salt, and lime juice.

Lima: Mexican lime (in Florida called key lime). Smaller, more fragrant and acidic, and thinner skinned that its Asian ancestor.

Masa harina: Mexican corn flour. The basis for *tortillas* and *tamales.* Aztecs, Zapotecs, and Mayas all used the nixtamalization process, i.e., soaking and cooking dried corn kernels with lime or wood ash. This enhanced the nutritional value and also made it easier to grind.

Mole: Mexico's famously elaborate sauce, made to accompany turkey, chicken, or pork, a moveable feast of ingredients (including dried fruit, nuts, spices, garlic, chilies, chocolate, shredded *tortilla*), cooked for several hours. Puebla and Oaxaca are the *mole* capitals, where there are countless variations.

Nopal: the leaf or paddle of the cactus that produces prickly pears. The spines are cut off and the leaf is sliced before being fried, grilled, or roasted. It is very nutritious; high in calcium, fiber, and vitamins A and C.

Orégano: Mexican oregano is used abundantly in the Yucatán. The subtle flavor resembles a mixture of sage and Italian oregano.

Recado: seasoning blends. The Yucatan's classic formula that comes in red (from the *achiote* seed), black (*chilmole,* from charred chilies), and green (from pumpkin seeds and oregano). *Recado para bistec* (for beef) contains black pepper, cinnamon, and coriander seeds.

Tamales: the Nahuatl word *tamal* literally means "wrapped," and that is what this ubiquitous *antojito* is, whether sweet or salty. Inside a dried corn husk or banana-leaf envelope is a soft corn dough filled with anything from turkey with *mole* to almonds and raisins – or even strawberries, allegedly another of Moctezuma's fancies. They are cooked by steaming and are a popular fiesta food with origins going back thousands of years.

Tomatillo: A small green fruit in a papery husk that has a tart edge, and is related to the Cape gooseberry. Canned and fresh *tomatillos* are available outside Mexico.

MEXICAN INGREDIENTS SUPPLIERS

Mexican ingredients are increasingly available at the big supermarkets, but for specialty items the suppliers below will send by mail order.

MexGrocer.com

4060 Morena Blvd., Suite C
San Diego, CA 92117
Tel: (877) 463-9476
Email: info@mexgrocer.com
www.mexgrocer.com

An online grocery store for hard-to-find, authentic Mexican food and spices. Offers more than 1,500 specialty Mexican products, including cooking tools.

El Mercado Latino

Pike Place Market
Seattle, WA 98101
Tel: (206) 223-9374 **Fax:** (206) 233-9440
Email: contact@latinmerchant.com
www.latinmerchant.com

Specializes in Latin foods and Latin food related products. Huge selection of spices, chili peppers, sweets, and more.

Melissa Guerra

4100 North 2nd, Suite 200
McAllen, TX 78504
Tel: (877) 875-2665 **Fax:** (956) 682-5101
Email: info@melissaguerra.com
www.melissaguerra.com

Small selection of quality, hard-to-find ingredients, including *piloncillo*.

GourtmetSleuth

PO Box 508
Los Gatos, CA 95031
Tel: (408) 354-8281
Email: helpme@gourmetsleuth.com
www.gourmetsleuth.com

Specializes in items not readily available, like molcajetes (Mexican stone, mortar and pestles), pot de creme cups, and tortilla presses. Also carries spices, chilies, and more.

Pacific Island Market, L.L.C.

2610 Breezy Point
O Fallon, MO 63368
Tel: (636) 272-0604
Email: sales@asiamex.com
www.asiamex.com

Large selection of ethnic food products, including a great selection of Mexican spices, chili peppers, and more.

Rancho Gordo

1755 Industrial Way, #26
Napa, CA 94558
Tel: (707) 259-1935
Email: info@ranchogordo.com
www.ranchogordo.com

Great selection of heirloom beans, spices, and more.

The Spice House

Online: www.thespicehouse.com
Tel: (847) 328-3711

Extensive selection of hard to find spices.

RECOMMENDED RESTAURANTS

Entries marked by an asterisk (*) signify restaurants featured in the book.

MEXICO CITY

*Aguila y Sol Emilio Castelar 229, Polanco
+ 52 55 5281 8354. A superbly theatrical backdrop for Martha Ortiz's delectable cuisine which exudes the soul of Mexico. Very upmarket and romantic.

Azul y Oro Centro Cultural Universitario, UNAM, Coyoacán + 52 55 5622 7135. Even if you're not a student, Ricardo Muñoz Zurita's university restaurant is gaining accolades fast. Weekdays only. He will soon open the more central **La Esmeralda**.

Bellinghausen Londres 95, Zona Rosa + 52 55 5207 6149 A timeless old classic serving excellent seafood and steaks. Like a French brasserie but with a verdant patio. Lunch only.

El Bajio Av. Cuitlahuac 2709, Colonia Obrero Popolar, Azcapotzalco + 52 55 5341 9889. Off the beaten track but Carmen "Titita" Ramirez Degollado is an ace of Xalapan (Veracruz) cooking, seconded by daughter Maria.

*El Tajín Centro Cultural Veracruzana, Av. Miguel Angel de Quevedo 687, Coyoacán + 52 55 5659 5759.
Alicia Gironella de'Angeli continues to wow with her delicious and impeccable Mexican menu.

Izote Presidente Masaryk 513, Polanco + 52 55 5280 1671. Patricia Quintana's gastro-temple offers exquisite *tamales* and *ceviches*. New twists with a French accent on old Mexican favorites.

*Naos Av. Palmas 425, Colonia Lomas de Chapultepec
+ 52 55 5520 5702. Owner-chef Mónica Patiño flits between her three restaurants, but you can rely on eating perfectly prepared fusion food based on Mexican classics.

*Pujol Petrarca 254, Polanco + 52 55 5545 4111.
Book well in advance to grab a table at this intimate, modern restaurant to join Enrique Olvera's gastro-voyage of discovery.

Restaurante Chon Regina 160 (Jesus María), Centro Historico + 52 55 5522 1070. A rare chance to indulge in pre-Hispanic tidbits such as maguey worms, iguana, grasshoppers, ants' eggs, and armadillo with mango.

Texka Hotel Royal, Amberes 78, Zona Rosa
+ 52 55 5228 9918. If you haven't been to Juan Mari Arzak's San Sebastian gastro-temple, then sample his Basque *nueva cocina* here. Formal and upmarket.

VERACRUZ

El Mesón Xiqueño Calle Miguel Hidalgo 148, Xico
+ 52 228 813 0781. Paco the parrot rules the colonial-style patio where you can tuck into appetizing local fare such as *empanadas* with goat's cheese and *jalapeño* chilies or *chilatole xiqueño*.

*La Fonda del Viejito Via Carranza 71, Xico
+ 52 228 129 8225. This is Flor and Pati's terrain down a side street by the town hall. Great nourishing fare from morning till night.

PUEBLA

Fonda de Santa Clara Calle 3 Poniente 307, Centro
+ 52 222 242 2659. A Pueblan institution since 1965. Quaint, cheerful, and one of three. Renowned for classics such as *chiles en nogada*, *mole poblano* and, in season, *huauzontles*, *escamoles*, and *huitlacoches*.

Hotel La Purificadora Callejon de la 10 Norte 802, Paseo de San Francisco, Puebla +52 222 309 1920. In this converted water-bottling plant (now a hotel designed by architect Ricardo Legorreta), Enrique Olvera's sublime, inventive Mexican *botanas* (like Spanish tapas) appeal to a hip clientele.

*Mesón de la Sacristía, Calle 6 Sur No. 304, Callejon de los Sapos, Centro Historico, Puebla + 52 222 242 3554 www.mesones-sacristia.com. Indulge in chef Alonso Hernández's cuisine on the patio of Puebla's original boutique hotel.

MICHOACAN

Cenaduria La Lupita Sanchez de Tagle 1004, Colonia Ventura Puente, Morelia + 52 443 312 1340. A popular local place just outside the main center.

*La Azotea Hotel Los Juaninos, Morelos Sur 39, Centro, Morelia + 52 443 312 0036 www.hoteljuaninos.com.mx. Ruben and his son Adrian keep the *platos* coming in Morelia's most scenic central restaurant.

*La Conspiración Morelos Norte 33, Esquina Av. Madero, Centro, Morelia + 52 443 317 6200. Friday and Saturday nights buzz till 2am.

Los Mirasoles Av. Madero Poniente 549, Esquina Leon Guzman, Centro, Morelia + 52 443 317 5777 www.losmirasoles.com. Morelian specialties such as pork in *pulque* marinade and homemade pasta in an elegant, colonial, patio setting.

OAXACA

*Casa Oaxaca Constitución 104a, Centro, Oaxaca + 52 951 514 4173. The must-do, must-eat place in Oaxaca. A lovely roof terrace overlooks the flank of Santo Domingo, while downstairs artworks harmonize with Alejandro Ruíz's epicurean *cocina*. Tasting menus of either *mole* or seafood.

Hacienda Los Laureles Hidlago 21, San Felipe del Agua + 52 951 501 5300. Escape to the hills! Beautiful lush garden surroundings for indulging in sophisticated Oaxacan and international dishes.

La Biznaga García Vigil 512, Centro, Oaxaca + 52 951 516 1800 www.labiznaga.org. Fun, young, and good organic fare, breaking a few salad, soup, and *quesadilla* boundaries.

La Casa de la Abuela Av. Hidalgo 616 Altos, Centro, Oaxaca + 52 951 516 3544. This is classic *mole* HQ and the best place to sample salty *chapulines* washed down with a margarita. Get a table with a view to make the most of the location.

*Los Danzantes Macedonio Alcala 403-404, Centro, Oaxaca + 52 951 501 1184/7 www.losdanzantes.com.mx. Superbly designed by Alejandro Dacosta with an open pool and soaring walls. Relish in Miguel Jiménez's cooking and seasonal menus.

*Restaurant Tlamanalli Av. Juarez 39, Teotitlán del Valle + 52 951 524 4006. Abigail Mendoza's family headquarters are where you'll experience sound Zapotec food with soul and smiles.

YUCATAN

*Hacienda Teya Km 12.5 Carretera Mérida-Cancun, Mérida + 52 999 988 0800/04 www.haciendateya.com. Lunch in hacienda splendor, just a 10-minute drive from Mérida, and savor Martiniano's authentic Yucatecan classics.

Hacienda Xcanatun Km 12 Carretera Mérida-Progreso www.xcanatun.com. The restaurant at this 18th-century hacienda hotel serves elegantly prepared French-Yucatán-Caribbean dishes.

La Casa de Frida Calle 61 526 x Calle 66, Centro, Mérida + 52 999 928 2311 www.lacasadefrida.com.mx. Soak up the Frida Kahlo atmosphere in this low-key patio restaurant. Excellent *chile en nogada* and *sopa azteca*.

*La Playita Celestun + 52 988 916 2052. With its interior murals, stuffed iguanas, and tables spilling onto the sand, La Playita is easily the most atmospheric of Celstun's seafront restaurants. *Ceviche* heaven in fact.

*Nectar Av. 1 no. 412, Int. 1, Colonia Diaz Ordaz, Mérida + 52 999 938 0838. Roberto Solis and Santiago Pineda Leyva's funky and modern restaurant in Mérida. Stunning food and service.

INDEX